More from THE TEXTILE ARTIST series

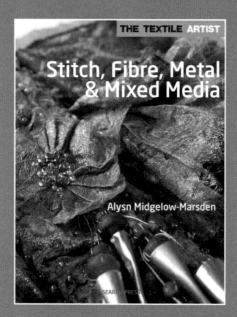

Stitch, Fibre, Metal &
Mixed Media
978-1-84448-762-2

Appliqué Art
978-1-84448-868-1

Felt &
Fibre Art

Felt & Fibre Art

A practical guide to making beautiful felted artworks

Val Hughes

SEARCH PRESS

First published in 2015

Search Press Limited
Wellwood, North Farm Road,
Tunbridge Wells, Kent TN2 3DR

Illustrations and text copyright © Val Hughes 2015

Photographs by Paul Bricknell at Search Press studios

Photographs and design copyright © Search Press Ltd. 2015

ISBN: 978-1-84448-992-3

The Publishers and author can accept no responsibility for any consequences arising from the information, advice or instructions given in this publication.

Suppliers
If you have difficulty in obtaining any of the materials and equipment mentioned in this book, then please visit the Search Press website for details of suppliers:
www.searchpress.com

You are invited to visit the author's website:
www.valhughes.com

Printed in China

ACKNOWLEDGEMENTS

My mum, Elizabeth Owens, for her constant support and guidance. She got me through my degree by sitting up with me, often sewing until the early hours without ever once complaining.

My children, Christian and Emma. Sorry about the scary mannequins in the living room. This is for you, so you can continue to love the things I love. I hope you can see why your home was always full of wool, fabrics and threads!

Roz Dace, whose enthusiasm about my work – not to mention her persistence – helped me to feel confident enough to envisage the work in print and agree to put pen to paper. I will never forget our long conversations in Covent Garden over coffee and cakes.

The wonderful team at Search Press, and especially Edward Ralph.

Martin Hinks, my partner, always encouraging me to love my achievements and to believe in myself. Without Martin this book would not have been written.

Front cover
A Fallen Rose
This textile art piece, and the Anne Boleyn collection from which it is taken, is detailed on pages 64–85.

Page 1
War of the Roses
Wearable felt art, taken from the Elizabeth Woodville collection detailed on pages 104–123.

Contents

Introduction

For as long as I can remember, I have always loved to sketch, paint and play around with fabrics. I see myself as fortunate to be from a family of artistic and creative people. My father, a joiner and carpenter, encouraged me to always look, listen and explore. The creative and exciting way he used to refer to natural events like the waves and appearance of rainbows stays with me. My mother, a dressmaker, was always working on clothes for my sister and me as we grew up. Back then I found the noise of the sewing machine annoying – even a little frightening – though at the same time I was attracted and fascinated by its potential.

My parents filled my childhood with magic and creativity, and both helped to instil a vivid appreciation of the world around me – the landscapes, the light, colours, the textures and proportion. All of these wonderful experiences have gone on to influence my style of working with textiles.

Creativity is such an important part of our psyche. It is what makes us different to any other living creature. It is my hope that the reader will come to see the beauty around us, often in things we would not automatically expect to be 'beautiful', and that this book will inspire people to find their own creativity, while enjoying a little bit of mine at the same time.

'I love colour, and drawing. My father told me many times
that my talent was a gift, one I should be careful not to
lose or waste.'

Materials

The following pages examine the materials and tools I use in my felt artwork. For the techniques and projects in this book, little space is needed, and no gadgetry more high tech than a simple sewing machine.

The wonderful thing about the materials for felt art is that they are all easily accessible. The wool I use can be found in numerous suppliers across the world, while the fabrics can be found online, in specialist suppliers, in markets, or even recycled from old curtains or garments. Similarly, all of the embellishments, from beads to silk fibres, can be easily sourced.

'Mark making is a rewarding and important element of the artistic process for me. Where I used a pencil or pen for my childhood sketches, in my felt making and embroidery I now make my marks with a needle!'

Wool fibres

Felt is at the heart of my artwork, and the wool fibres from which felt is made are the most fundamental material of all. These are generally bought as 'tops', semi-processed wool that has been cleaned and combed into coils of wool called hanks or skeins.

Merino wool

The merino is a breed of sheep that comes from central Spain and is prized for its wool. It provides us with some of the finest and softest wool of any sheep breed. It is breathable and odour resistant, and various different grades of merino wool are available.

I love using merino wool because if felts extremely well, creating a flat, even surface which can be successfully embellished or machine embroidered. It also readily enables the addition of other embellishments – using tiny slivers of merino wool fibres on the top surface to lock in pieces of lace, braids, skeletal leaves and knitting wools, to give just a few examples.

Merino wool tops can be mixed readily and to good effect, giving a lovely painterly look to your work. They are ideal for the beginner to use because they shrink quickly, which speeds up the felting process.

'I love working with merino wool tops – the feel and smell of them are wonderful! The array of colours available is pleasing to the eye; and carefully teasing and laying out the fibres can be very therapeutic.'

Other wools

Soft wool tops like merino are sensual and very 'moreish', but using different wools instead of, or in addition to, merino tops can add interest and variety to your felting.

British wools

Britain, where I live, has more than sixty breeds of sheep, many of which provide excellent quality wool tops that are tactile and fun to use! The qualities of some of my favourite varieties are described below:

Bluefaced Leicester The natural colours of this breed's lustrous and silky wool are quite beautiful. It produces soft wools useful for knitwear and blends for fine cloth.

Shetland Soft and silky Shetland, with its natural colours of browns, blacks and greys, can be used to make excellent shawls, Fair Isle knitwear and soft woven fabrics.

Wensleydale A silky wool which has a creamy white colour. Used primarily as a knitting yarn or for upholstery. It is great for embellishment because it is so curly.

Suffolk A creamy white wool that is soft and fine in texture. It is hard-wearing but can be difficult to felt and spin on its own, so it is usually used in blends for knitwear and cloth.

Welsh Mountain Mainly used in tweeds, blankets and carpets, Welsh Mountain is a coarse wool that is hard to felt, but worth the effort for the wonderful texture it adds to your work.

Knitting wools and yarns

I often add knitting wools and yarns to my work to add texture and interest. I usually combine knitting wools with hand-rolled felt or nuno felt (see page 34), but I also couch it – either by hand or using the sewing machine – onto fabric, sometimes trapping it between layers of fabric.

Knitting wool This can range from a pure new wool, merino lambswool, aran to cotton or silk blends. I use this wool both for its texture and the added interest of colour.

Pure wool slub This yarn is great for adding texture. I also use knitting yarns containing viscose, often to give lustre to my work. Viscose is produced from pine wood pulp, which makes it an eco-friendly fibre – always a good thing!

Glitter effect yarn I occasionally use yarn that has a glitter effect. This is useful if you want to add a shimmer to your work.

Mohair, cotton and silk knitting wools All of these combine well and are good for adding to handmade felt projects.

'Be adventurous with knitting yarns. They can transform a piece of work into something really interesting, textured and colourful.'

Mixed and unusual wools

I have recently begun to experiment with merino wool mixed with vegetable fibres and other types of fleece.

Soy bean fibre A vegetable-based fibre, this complements other fibres, such as merino wool, and has a gorgeous lustre giving it a silk like appearance. It can be dyed because it is very strong and robust.

Bamboo fibre Made from bamboo pulp, the fibres of this wool are white, silky and extremely soft. It blends well with other fibres, such as wool tops and silk cocoon strippings. It can also be dyed.

Alpaca fleece I occasionally mix alpaca fleece in with other wool. Good quality alpaca fibre is luxurious – fine and soft. Although it does not dye well, it can be bought in gorgeous natural shades of white, browns, greys, fawn and black. Its quality can vary from coarse to very fine.

Silk fibres

Silk will not felt on its own, and needs to be mixed with felt fibres. It gives a lift to felt, which can appear a little flat when made from wool alone.

Working with silk fibres is an extremely soothing and positive experience, and I frequently use silk when felt-making.

Mulberry silk Like wool, this is bought as tops. Mulberry silk is soft and lustrous. It is naturally bright and white as a result of the silkworms having been fed mulberry leaves.

Tussah silk Another natural silk bought as tops, it is produced by tussah moths. The tops are often creamy in colour and sometimes a darker shade resembling tea. This type of silk adds a natural golden contrast to the work.

Silk noils Found in the inner parts of the silkworm cocoon. These are shorter fibres that can be particularly useful in creating added texture.

OTHER SILKS

I also use silk handkerchief, where the fibres are laid flat; mawata bonnets or caps, which are curved layers of silk fibres. Another kind of silk is throwster's waste. This is stranded filaments of silks, often with sticky gum remaining amongst the fibres.

'It fascinates me that a caterpillar can produce such a beautiful material as the protective and life-enhancing – for the silkworm, at least – silk cocoon.'

Handmade papers

An abundance of gorgeous handmade papers, including those made from banana fibres, mulberry silk, waste papers, and even those like lotka paper (made from bark and papyrus) can be purchased from specialist suppliers.

Papers can be used with your felt artwork to create mixed media pieces, but they can also be used on their own for wall hangings. I tear, cut and distress my papers before stitching them into my work.

Paper pulp Paper can be made from old letters, non-shiny envelopes and other paper waste by soaking them, beating them into a pulp, then laying them out flat on a wire mesh before leaving them to dry.

Mulberry and tussah silk The art of creating silk paper is ancient, dating back to 1500BC. The resulting paper is so versatile – you can stitch into it, mould it, incorporate it into collages, and, of course, paint on it. Silk papers from mulberry and tussah silk tops can be purchased from specialist retailers, or they can be handmade. Unlike paper made from silk strippings, this requires adhesive paste, net and drying time. This process is therefore a lengthy one, but the resulting paper will be of high quality.

Plant pulp While handmade paper is most commonly made from recycled paper pulp, sheets can also be created from plant matter like onion skins, cabbage leaves, iris leaves, reeds or the stringy stalks of rhubarb and sunflowers. Unfortunately, it is quite rare to find plant pulp-based paper in shops, and to make this kind of paper requires washing soda and boiling to break down the plant matter. Although I have done this in the past and love reusing and recycling in this way, I rarely have the time these days to pursue it.

Silk paper from strippings I often add silk cocoon strippings (also known as gummy silk) to my mixed media pieces. Strippings contain a natural adhesive, so wetting the fibres and ironing them between baking parchment will produce 'paper' with a distinctive fabric feel. This can then be embellished with various threads, leaves, knitting wools, heat-fusible iridescent fibres, skeletal leaves and can be easily stitched into either by hand or by machine. It can also be folded and shaped to create three-dimensional forms.

Fabrics

I like to apply wool fibres to fabric to create nuno felt (see page 34). My favourite fabrics, described below, all possess a wonderful draping quality. I embellish them with free machine embroidery, and also distress them for use with felt.

Chiffon This woven lightweight fabric is sheer in appearance. It has a slight stretch and can feel a little rough on its surface. It can be made from cotton, silk or synthetic fibres; and is a lovely fabric to use for evening wear, giving an elegant, draping quality.

Silk chiffon Ideal for using with wool fibres and mulberry silks in nuno felt making techniques. I also like to use silk chiffon when stitching and overlaying different fabrics. It frays easily and gives a natural organic feel to the work, often puckering up quite naturally adding texture and variation to the finished piece. Silk chiffon is also fabulous for making nuno scarves, wraps and even jackets and gilets.

Cotton muslin A loosely woven fabric, cotton muslin has been traded since the time of the ancient Greeks. It originates from Bengal, but became very popular in France at the end of the eighteenth century. This is largely because it is lightweight, cool and breathable. It also very inexpensive, and as such is often used by dress makers to create a toile (a test for a fitted garment). I use cotton muslin primarily to create scarves and wraps, usually using the nuno felt method as the wool fibres readily adhere to the fabric. On occasions I have dyed them with inks and cheap cold water and washing machine dyes to make a variegated cloth which can later be machine embroidered.

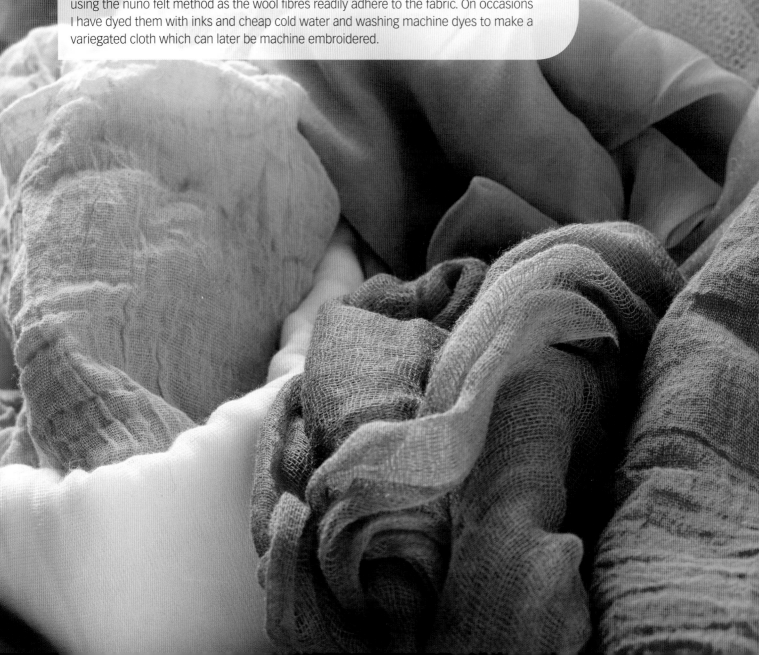

Cotton scrim Very similar to muslin, cotton scrim has a more open weave and is extremely lightweight. It is ideal for nuno felting, giving very interesting effects as the wool fibres lock on to its open weave and shrink, puckering and distressing the fabric beautifully.

Organza Organza is a lightweight, sheer fabric which I have occasionally used in my work. A synthetic fibre, organza tends to be used for evening wear, bridal wear and interiors. It comes in a vast array of colours as well as plain and two tone. It can be purchased already embroidered. However, I like to use plain organza and then embroider it myself using free machine embroidery techniques.

Crystal organza Similar to organza, crystal organza has a more marked sparkle effect which can be useful if you want to achieve a shimmer and shine in your work.

Other fabrics I also like to use voiles which are sheer fabrics as well as other 'found' materials and those from other projects, left over and therefore recyclable. These add colour and texture as well as being good for distressing, leaving raw edges and loose threads.

TIP: TRY CHEAPER ALTERNATIVES

It is always good to experiment. For example, I have found success in applying wool tops to a polyester chiffon – a much cheaper alternative to silk chiffon.

Embellishments

Threads Using different threads can add interest, texture and colour to both machine and hand embroidery. Cotton and silk threads are useful for construction and mark making, while metallic and pearlised threads are fun for adding lustre and sheen. Hand embroidery threads lend themselves to fine, detailed work. Threads left loose or suspended can add a natural, unfinished, organic look to your work. Threads are so exiting and so very versatile. Experimentation with threads makes for interesting results.

Iridescent fibres Iridescent fibres are fine reflective fibres that add sparkle to your work. They are useful for holding other mixed media materials – such as knitting wools, leaves and threads – in place. Subtlety is the key with these fibres: a little goes a long way! The material comes in a variety of different colours and some is heat-bondable. This can be heat-fixed (in a well-ventilated room) using an iron and then cut into shapes. Over-ironing can change the colour and result in a loss of shine/glow.

Beads Available in a vast selection of different shapes, sizes and materials – paper, glass, felt and bone, to name just a few – beads add light, texture or colour. I prefer to use smaller, more subtle beads. Try visiting local charity shops and recycling the beads from old jewellery to give your work more meaning and a little bit of history – and it's environmentally friendly, too.

'I love to use natural and organic materials in my artwork. Petals, seeds, leaves, natural dyes and even tea stains are all useful embellishments.'

Paint Watered-down and added to fabric, acrylic paints add a wash of colour. Applied more thickly, texture can be added to your work by drawing a comb or pencil through the paint, dabbing it with a sponge or indenting with an old cotton reel. Watercolour paints can also be used.

Leaves Autumn time is brilliant for collecting leaves. I like to incorporate skeletal leaves into my felt and handmade paper. Care has to be taken not to crush them during felt making, but, with a little patience and practice, they can be very useful. Sometimes I simply stitch them onto fabric using free machine embroidery. I usually buy skeletal leaves, but you can create your own by using baking soda to strip the leaf leaving behind its skeleton. Waxy leaves such as magnolia, maple and hydrangea work the best.

Oil sticks These sticks, ideal for adding colour quickly and efficiently to large areas, come in a range of vivid colours, including metallic. Oil-based, they are produced with a thick cardboard barrel to hold.

Felting materials

These materials are essential to the main technique in this book – wet felting.

Soap The use of soap is primarily to speed up the process of felting. The type you use in wet felting does not really matter. It can be a traditional bar of soap, washing-up liquid added to a spray bottle, or even soap flakes sprinkled onto your work before applying the water. My preference is to use a bar of olive oil soap which is biodegradable and kinder to both the fibres and your hands.

Spray bottle Used for dispersing water evenly over the fibres, spray bottles can be purchased from specialist felting suppliers or garden centres, but I tend to simply thoroughly rinse out an old kitchen cleaner spray bottle and use that.

Towel and plastic sheeting These are used to protect your work surface. The towels soak up most of the water from the felting process, while the plastic sheeting prevents any excess water leaking through.

Rolling mat Specialist felting mats offer an effective way to speed up the felting process. They give a firm base when working and make rolling easier than the alternatives (such as using bubble wrap). However, bamboo mats – often sold as place mats or sushi mats – are inexpensive and just as good!

Netting Netting is used to cover the laid-out felt before it is felted. It helps to keep the wool in place as you roll the work. You can buy netting from specialist fabric shops, but charity stores often sell net curtains which can be cut to size.

Other materials

Sewing machine I use a sewing machine to add decorative stitching to my artwork with the free machine embroidery technique, using the needle like a paintbrush or pencil. More expensive computerised machines are available that can do preset decorative stitches, which can be useful, but as long as your machine does a basic straight stitch, it will be fine.

Iron An iron is essential when using heat-fusible fabrics, but it can also be used for creating silk papers or stiffening felt fabric. I keep an old one in my studio especially for craft projects.

Sewing needles I do not tend to be all that particular about the needles I use for stitching felt together or for the embellishment of my felt. However, when working on sheer fabrics and for finer, more delicate free machine embroidery work, it is essential to use needles that have been specifically made for this purpose. Replace these needles often to avoid snagging fabrics and also prevent frequent thread breakages.

Felting needles These are specialist needles which are extremely sharp. They have small metal barbs lower down their length which push and lock wool fibres together. These needles enable you to create finer detail on many and varied felting projects. Felting needles come in different sizes, referred to as 'gauge'; the higher the gauge, the finer the needle. I tend to use 36 gauge needles. Felting needles can be purchased with a wooden handle, and also as a multi-needle tool. The latter can be useful if you want to build up large areas quickly. For finer detail, where more control is required, use a single needle. Felting needles can break quite easily – so a good supply will likely be necessary.

Felting pad Used when needle felting, this pad is placed underneath your felt piece or fibres. Made from dense foam rubber, it provides a backing for your needle to poke into after it has been pushed through the felt and fibres. This allows you to apply the fibres and extra detail without the risk of breaking a needle against a hard surface. Specialist foam pads and brushes are available but these often prove quite expensive. I find upturned dense bristle brushes or foam seat pads (available from DIY shops) good alternatives as long as they are dense and at least 5cm (2in) in depth.

Cookie cutters I like to use cookie cutters to help me create defined shapes when needle felting – the fibres are placed within and needle felted in place, enabling you to create shapes quickly as well as adding a degree of protection for your fingers. They are available in many shapes such as hearts, stars, moons and teddy bears. Cookie cutters can be either plastic or metal; both will work equally well.

Soluble fabric There are many types of soluble fabric on the market, some that work in hot water, some in cold. Personally I prefer the cold water soluble variety which allows the quick dissolving of fabric underneath a cold tap, leaving your threaded fabric in place. It is essential to make sure all soluble fabric is removed otherwise it will dry hard and once dried it is much harder to remove.

Baking parchment I have included this because it is an essential component of the creation of silk cocoon papers. It is important that the baking parchment is non-stick and silicone treated. If not, your cocoon strippings will simply stick to it and will be impossible to remove. Note: baking parchment is not the same as greaseproof paper!

Plastic carrier bags I never throw plastic carrier bags away. They can prove very useful when pressing and rubbing wet fibres together in the felting process. I have also started using plastic carrier bags in my projects themselves: I place the plastic between two pieces of baking parchment before applying a hot iron to melt and therefore fuse the plastic. I suggest you take great care here in terms of ensuring adequate ventilation. Although most plastic bags will not give off excess fumes, manufacturing techniques may change from time to time and it is never a good idea to be too flippant about the chemicals within the plastics we may be using. Be aware that some plastics are capable of reaching high temperatures, so take great care when removing fused bags from the parchment.

'I have used a lot of different sewing machines but always come back to my absolute favourite: a compact, robust and reliable machine that has been in my family for more years than I can remember. I have put everything under its needle and foot – from gorgeous fabrics to plastic, paper and even wax!'

Getting started

Inspiration

As an artist and teacher, it is my firmly-held belief that every student or reader has an innate ability to explore, and to utilise their own experiences and individual beliefs to inspire beautiful artwork. From our own personal inspiration, we can go on to express ourselves through our art and our creativity. If by doing this we inspire others – even in a small way – what a fantastic legacy we leave!

The first stage is to work out what inspires you. Inspiration is all around; from objects around you to your emotional response to an event. Fleeting images and impressions can spark ideas that you can develop or that lead you on to other ideas. If you are struggling for inspiration, the following suggestions provide some paths to get you started.

Use your senses

Get out in the fresh air. A beach can conjure many inspirational visuals: patterns in sand, salt-encrusted driftwood or perhaps a fish thrown up by a passing storm, its scales shining in the sunlight. On a woodland walk you might encounter spiders' webs, new-formed dewdrops, fungi, frost-enveloped branches or sunlight shining through trees and branches. Do not restrict yourself to conventionally beautiful images – sometimes sights like paint peeling from a door or the patterns on dry stone walls that separate fields can provide you with inspiration.

Travelling can be a great resource for inspiration. Having access to different cultures and ways of life has introduced lots of colours and textures which have stayed with me to this day. In addition, there is no reason inspiration cannot be drawn from non-visual senses such as touch, taste or smell. Thinking of my time in the Middle East and North Africa brings to mind many different sensations: heat hazes, aromatic spices, bustling human activity and dialogue, different fabrics, mosaic pattern works and hot, bright colours that evoke feelings of warmth. Again, do not just look to the conventional for inspiration – even camel skeletons in the desert can serve as inspiration.

Emotions

Much of my work is a mixture of sensual impressions and the deeper, emotional reactions to those. The feelings caused by experiences of loss, death and bereavement, injustices and violations can be powerful sources of inspiration; and those seemingly negative feelings can often create powerful works of art. Of course, positive emotions are also a valuable source of inspiration. A happy day and a feeling of elation can inspire a lively and colourful piece that goes on to inspire others.

Literature and artefacts

Reading stories and poems can promote creativity and inspiration, as can photographs, pieces of music or memorabilia collected along our life journey. Dig out those old photograph albums and listen to your favourite songs to help inspire you.

My influences

To build on my thoughts on inspiration (see page 22), I thought it would be instructive to give you some examples of my own influences, and talk you through some of the practical aspects of how to go about recording and developing abstract images and feelings into physical pieces of textile artwork.

As a child, I kept books full of bark rubbings, lists of how many starlings or blackbirds I had seen that day, and sketches of day-to-day natural phenomena that had touched me. Family holidays and day trips tended to be seaside ones, and the activities – sailing, fishing, walks and cockle picking – were great sources of material. When walking, I picked berries and soft fruit, and took home leaves to press and preserve them.

As I grew up, I developed an interest in history – particularly ancient cultures and daily living – which gradually encroached on my creative thinking. In particular, I became drawn to the Tudor period. I began to read books about important women in history, and became interested in the six wives of King Henry VIII of England. Studying them led me to frequent trips into London and the surrounding area to see important landmarks associated with them, such as the Tower of London and Hever Castle in Kent. At times I felt I was being introduced to tortures, injustices towards people who did not fit in or who were made scapegoats. I found this so interesting, but it disturbed me at the same time. This was likely the embryonic stage of my interest in gender issues and the role of women in our society, a theme I explore in much of my work.

My interest in travel, other cultures and their ideas and artistry, was another crucial element in my artistic development. The first of my trips abroad as a sixteen-year-old was to Majorca. I identified sand, sea and architecture as central themes; and was interested in the differences in the climate and lifestyle from my home in Britain. I looked at how different stones and colours were used, and the region's decorative pottery. The overlap of old and new together with its association to history and archaeology was cemented in my mind.

Shown on these pages are some photographs showing the variety of places and objects from which I draw my inspiration. I take my camera everywhere. It's a great tool for capturing a moment and will help you to quickly build up your own visual resource of inspirational imagery.

Identifying your influences

Your influences will be as diverse as mine, and it can seem difficult to know where to begin. A good place to start is simply to learn to look around you. Take time to see how the clouds quickly change shape. See how the leaves and fields change colours through the seasons. Carry a small sketchbook or camera with you. In this way anything you see that catches your interest can be recorded.

Just thinking about seemingly everyday experiences can help you to find what subconsciously affects and influences you. Why not think about a recent shopping trip. What patterns and colours influenced your purchases? Learn to recognise what gives you pleasure and what stimulates other emotions such as calmness, or anger. Your holiday snaps are a whole resource of imagery that can invoke memories of happiness or pleasure, and images of the sun, sea, sand, and architecture you saw. You could think about big celebrations or events such as Halloween, Christmas, Easter, or birthdays. What comes to mind when you imagine these events? Was it the cakes and candles, ghosts and ghouls, colourful fireworks or maybe the fairy on top of the Christmas tree. Do you have a favourite book or story? Try to work out what it is about it that holds your interest. In this way you will be constantly evaluating and reviewing your own preferred influences and experiences.

It is important not to always view pieces of work or collections in isolation. Rather, it may be that you allow certain pieces of work that have inspired you to go on to influence and inspire other work or collections. Many of my textile art collections have links to one another that were not necessarily envisaged at the outset. For example, my *Anne Boleyn* collection on pages 64–85 led very quickly to another two collections entitled *The Haunting* and *Nightcrow*, which share some of the same themes. Similarly, the *Abracadabra* collection, some of which you can see on pages 86–103, began as deconstructed and reconstructed costumes from some of the work in *The Haunting*. Pieces from *Water, Snow and Ice* were partly influenced by the Pennine landscape, which led me in turn to think about the War of the Roses, and along came my *Elizabeth Woodville* work. Elizabeth also has a link to Anne Boleyn – Elizabeth was Henry VIII's grandmother and Anne was married to Henry.

Thoughts related to magic and dreams underpin my *Abracadabra* work, which in turn links nicely with *Alice in Wonderland*, as do the red roses that feature so heavily in the Lewis Carroll stories. The red rose again links back to both Anne Boleyn and Elizabeth Woodville. The interconnected nature of your influences will help you to explore yourself through your work.

Reference and design

Once you have fixed upon a point of inspiration, the next stage is to begin the practical aspects of designing your artwork. Much will depend on your theme – and, of course, your medium. My work focus is on wool fibres and felt, free machine embroidery and mixed media, so my design work takes this into account. Visual studies – such as sampling – will give you lots of ideas of how to develop your initial idea towards a successful outcome. To put it simply, observation and learning to look closely are the keys to good design. Follow up on those by translating what you have seen into drawing and sketches.

Observation and research

With your theme in mind, find books on the subject to read and related places to visit. For example, if sunlight on leaves is your inspiration, visit nearby woodlands, and check your local library for books on the trees you want to include. Research is essential in capturing colour, texture and detail. Build up a body of work by making sketches, taking photographs and sampling the area around your inspiration.

Translating your ideas into materials

Once you have done your research, think about the practical aspects of realising your work. Develop your ideas by choosing fabrics and threads that are appropriate to your initial designs. Choose whether to use threads, beads, fibres (or something else entirely) to interpret the pencil or paint marks on your sketches. Similarly, patterns from your existing body of work can be developed into embroidery or needle felting on a new piece. I like to use fibres in a painterly way and use the needle as I would a paintbrush or pencil. Referring to your notes and sketches at this stage can help you to choose materials.

Experiment and make samples

Once you have made some decisions on the materials you will use, make samples. Use different media such as wax crayons, inks, tissue paper, or cut and torn papers. Even simple blot painting and potato and sponge printing can help you to sort out your ideas into a workable order before embarking on the use of your final fabrics and threads.

This is a very important stage because, as mentioned above, an initial idea might not prove to be the best way forward – by making a few different samples, you will be able to ensure you are working with the materials that work best for you before you embark on the final piece.

TIP: NEW IDEAS

Sometimes a failed experiment can produce something unexpectedly useful. One of my students insisted on using polyester chiffon for a nuno project. The result was a gorgeous piece of cobweb felt which easily came away from the base fabric. Lovely but not nuno! While this was not the result she wanted, such experiments can spark new ideas of their own.

Key guidelines

- Observe.
- Make notes.
- Sketch.
- Trust your creative self.

All of this will help you to choose materials to go with your inspiration.

Colour

Colour is more than merely pigmentation. It means different things to different people, and has different meanings between cultures.

Some artists prefer to deliberately use a limited colour palette – i.e. only a small number of colours. Others may choose to work with a wider palette. Similarly, some prefer more muted tones, others brighter. Colour can be used naturalistically or interpretatively in your work, so do not feel you have to present things exactly as they appear.

Colour temperature and tone

Even when using a limited colour range, interest can be added by using 'warm' and 'cool' colour relationships. Reds, yellows and oranges tend to make us think of fire, sun and heat, while greens, blues and purples tend to make us think of sky, water and ice. The associations you make with a colour are important to interpreting your emotional response, which can influence whether you choose to describe a colour as warm or cool.

By progressing through tones and shades of a colour – starting with a pale blue then working towards a dark blue, for example – you can create atmosphere and mood and help to add texture and depth to your work.

Choosing a colour palette

Good use of colour will improve any finished piece, but choosing a palette can be intimidating. The key is not to be too hung up on your choices of colour, and instead to open up your mind and eyes to the range of different colours and tones within everyday objects. Colour changes with weather, light and perspective. For example, the sea changes from dark green to pale green, from grey to black, from dark blue to turquoise.

As with design, keeping sketchbooks, photographs, samples and notes of all your 'colour findings' will help you to appreciate different effects within the different fabrics, fibres and colours. In turn, this will help you work out which colours you will use for a piece of artwork.

Choosing colours to go with your inspiration and initial ideas has to be a very personal thing, and will undoubtedly be influenced by a number of factors unique to you.

Colour in my collections

My own collections tend to use a limited colour palette. In the *Anne Boleyn* collection, for example, I use red, black and hints of gold. These evoke the macabre and death-related context of Anne's final days. Hints of gold suggest Anne's nobility, the red links to her miscarriages and gruesome beheading, and the black suggests depression, death and the unknown.

In contrast, my more recent collections, *Abracadabra* and *Alice in Wonderland*, use a broader, brighter palette of colour to complement and enhance the bright and cheerful 'magical' themes of these collections.

Key guidelines

- Colours change all the time due to light, atmosphere and conditions.
- Different colours and tones can be seen within the same subject.
- Be aware of how colours interact with each other.
- Follow your intuition to make your choices.
- Make samples and notes before making your final decisions on a colour palette for your work.
- Cool colours create the impression of distance.
- Warm colours appear closer to the viewer.

Techniques

This chapter explains the four main techniques that are at the heart of my work: wet felting, nuno felting, needle felting and free machine embroidery. It is important for you to know these techniques if you want to embark on any of the projects that follow because they are used in all of the pieces in my collections which underpin and inform the individual projects.

Wet felting

Felt has been around for a long time. Some examples date back to 600BC, preserved by the sub-zero temperatures in the Siberian tombs in which they were found. Despite its age, felt remains as versatile and useful as ever. Some Mongolian tribes continue to live in traditional felted huts called yurts.

The process of wet felting involves adding warm water and soap to wool fibres and rolling and rubbing them together. Each wool fibre has tiny scales and when water and soap are added the scales swell up and begin to move about. The friction caused by agitating the fibres encourages the fibres to lock together into the robust fabric we call felt.

Felt can be made to be thick or thin, depending on how many layers of fibres you use. The thickness should be based upon how strong you need the finished felt to be, and its purpose. For my artwork, I generally use three layers.

Laying out the wool

1 Lay a sheet of plastic on your surface, then cover that with a towel. Place your rolling mat on top, then tease out the wool fibres from the end of the hank. Lay them out in a fine, even layer, with the fibres all lying in the same direction.

2 Lay down a second layer on top, with the fibres at right angles to the layer below. Lay out the handfuls so they overlap like tiles on a roof.

3 Continue to add overlapping layers of wool at right angles to the layer below. For a good, robust piece of felt, you need at least three layers.

4 To add decoration and interest, you can tease lengths of different-coloured wools and roll the fibres between your fingers, then lay them down in shapes; in this case, spirals and lines.

Initial rolling

5 Cover the wool, using a piece of netting big enough to cover the fibres completely and some of the surrounding area. Use a spray bottle filled with hot water to wet down the fibres thoroughly.

6 Holding the netting in place, draw the soap across the surface.

7 Carefully roll up the mat, with the netting and wool in place.

8 Place the palms of your hands on top of the rolled-up mat and rub back and forth vigorously to start felting the fibres. As a rough guide, I like to roll back and forth a hundred times, which sounds a lot; but passes quickly!

TIP: WETTING THE WOOL EVENLY

After applying the soap, you can rub a scrunched-up plastic carrier bag over the surface to help ensure the water is spread throughout the wool.

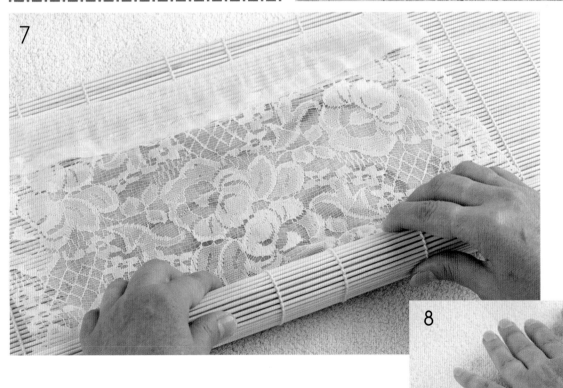

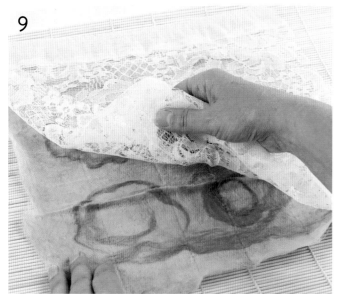

9

Checking the felt

9 Unroll the mat, and gently peel away the netting. The fibres should remain mostly in place.

10 If any ridges are revealed, lift the fibre away from the mat, ease out the creases a little by pulling gently on the sides, turn it ninety degrees and lie it back down flat on the mat. This is to prevent it from shrinking in one direction only.

11 Roll up the felt in the mat and repeat the rolling. Again, aim for around a hundred back-and-forth rolls.

12 Unroll the mat, turn the piece of felt through ninety degrees again, ease out any creases or thicker areas, and repeat the rolling.

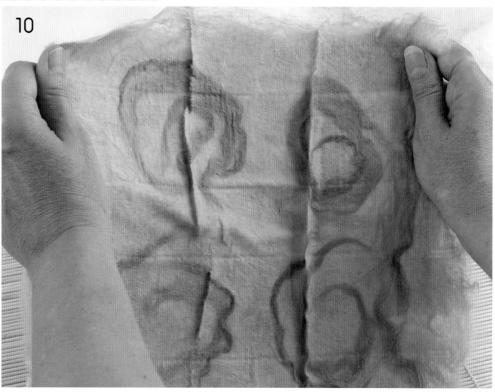

10

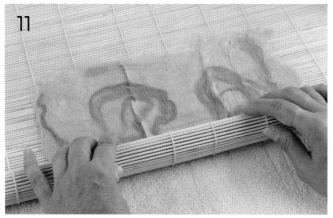

11

12

Finishing the felt

13 Continue rolling and turning the piece of felt. As you continue to work, the piece of felt will get smaller and smaller as the fibres lock together.

14 Rinse the piece of felt out in clean water, then wring it out thoroughly. Pull it back into shape and leave it to dry naturally. The inset shows the texture for which you should aim.

13

> ## TIP: CHECKING THE FINISHED FELT
>
> *A good way to check if the fibres have locked together is to rub the corner of the work between your forefinger and thumb. If the fibres move around, you need to continue rolling. If they stay together firmly, your piece is ready to rinse out.*

14

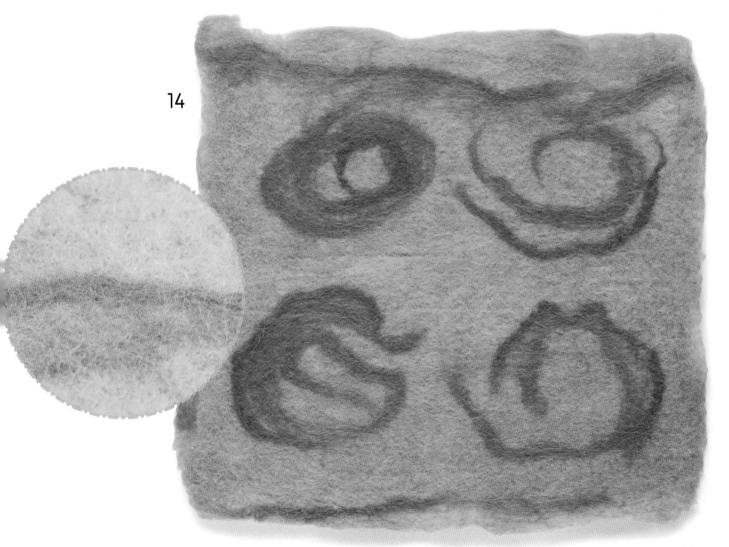

Nuno felting

Nuno felting is the process by which we encourage wool fibres to lock onto a piece of open weave cloth. This gives a luxurious, textured, draping quality to your felting. It is ideal for wearables, particularly shawls, scarves, wraps and also interior design wall hangings. The name comes from the Japanese word *nuno*, which means 'open weave cloth'.

The technique works best with natural fabrics such as cotton muslin, scrim or silk chiffon. The wool does not bond well to the smooth fibres of synthetic cloth, so always test out the fabric you wish to use before you begin.

It is important to rinse out or wet your fabric using warm water before use. This ensures that any 'dressing' or chemical used by the manufacturer is rinsed or diluted away. If dressing is left in your fabric it can hinder the process by which the fibres lock onto the cloth.

Laying out and preparing the wool

1 Lay a sheet of plastic on your surface, cover it with a towel, then place your rolling mat on top. Lay the fabric onto the mat, ensuring there is at least 3cm (1¼in) of the mat around all sides, then wet the fabric thoroughly. Tease out wool fibres from the hank very finely and lay them on top for a wispy effect.

2 Lay extra fibres around the edges of the fabric to prevent raw edges in the finished piece. Unlike normal wet felting, the wisps of wool do not have to create a complete layer; nor do they have to lie in the same direction as one another.

3 Lay netting over the top of the piece. Use a piece of netting large enough to completely cover it, along with some space around the outside. Using a spray bottle filled with tepid water, wet the wool tops thoroughly.

4 Hold the netting in place and draw the soap across the surface.

Rolling and tidying the wool

5 Roll up the mat, with the netting and wool in place. Place the palms of your hands on top of the rolled-up mat and rub back and forth vigorously to start felting the fibres, exactly as for normal wet felting. It is best to check your work more frequently when nuno felting – every fifty rolls, rather than every hundred as for wet felting – in order to avoid the risk of the fibres locking onto the netting as well.

6 Unroll the mat and carefully peel away the netting. Work gradually, and smooth any fibres that have locked into the netting back onto the felt.

7 At the edges, fold the wool under the raw edge (see inset); then lay the piece down flat on the mat again and rewet the edges using the spray bottle.

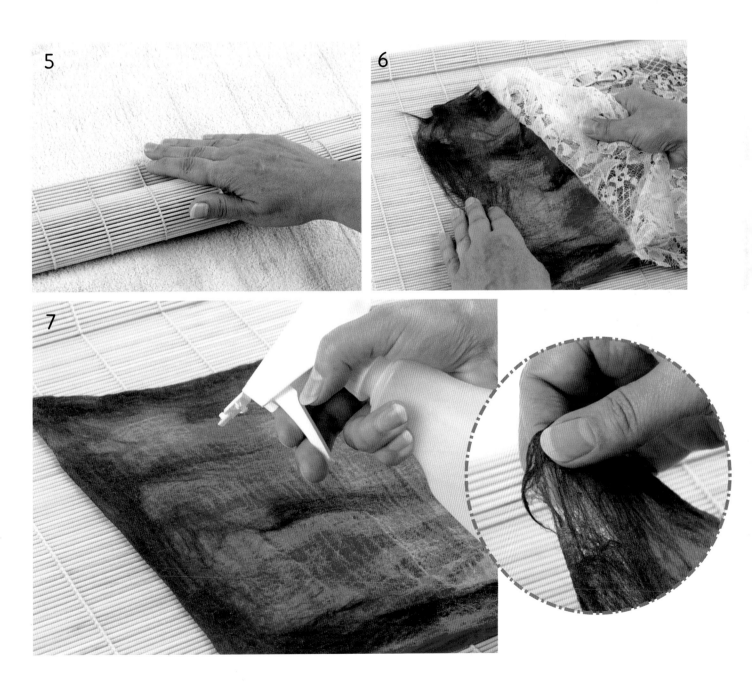

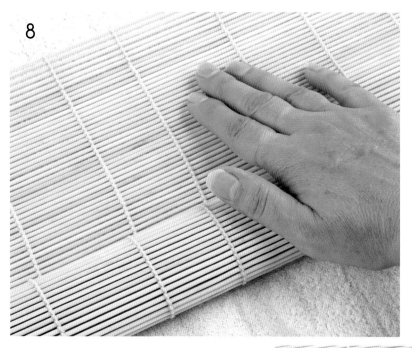

8

Tightening the felt

8 Roll the mat back up and repeat the rolling back and forth motion. With the netting removed, you can rub a hundred times now.

9 Unroll the mat periodically, lift the piece away from the mat and replace it before repeating the rolling. If you want the piece to shrink evenly, turn it through ninety degrees each time. If you want it to shrink in a particular direction (for example, if you are making a long scarf), there is no need to turn it as often.

10 Check to see if the threads are felting to the material by turning the piece over, looking for a puckered appearance (see inset) to the original fabric, and seeing if the fibres have come through to the back by pinching with your finger and thumb and drawing upwards.

TIP: WATER TEMPERATURE

For nuno felting, use only tepid water until the fibres begin to show on the back of the work. Once the fibres are revealed through the back of the cloth, you can speed up the process of tightening the felt by using hot water.

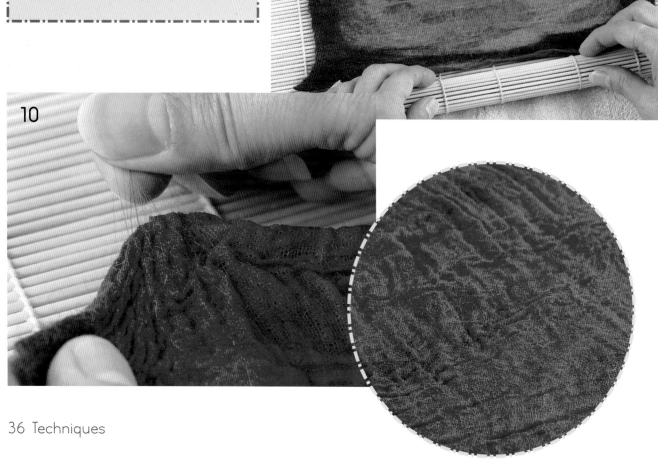

9

10

Finishing the felt

11 Once the wool is locked to the fabric, you can add heat to speed the process. You can rub the piece vigorously in your hands or spray it with hot water and continue rolling it in the mat.

12 Once the felt has shrunk to the size and texture you wish, rinse out the soap, wring the piece thoroughly, reshape it and leave it to dry. The inset detail shows a close-up of the puckered fabric from the front of the work.

'The fibres lock into the fabric and draw it in, giving nuno felted fabric a distinctive puckered appearance.'

11

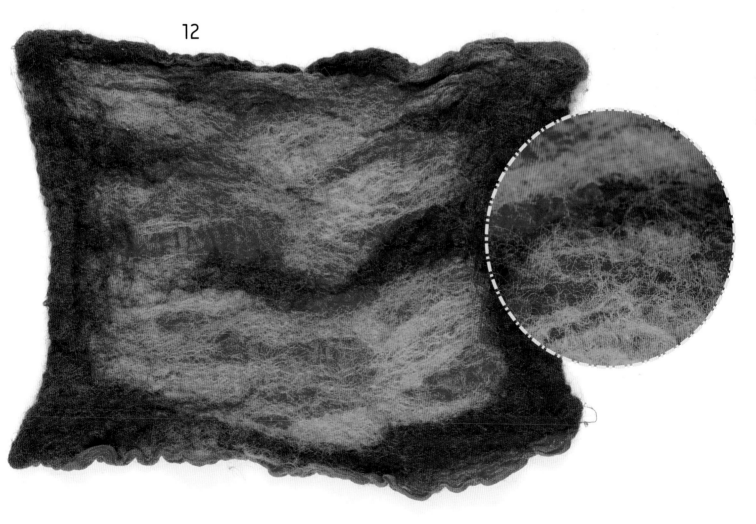

12

Needle felting

Felting with needles was originally developed for making felt on an industrial scale to be used in the motor and locomotive industries. It was produced on large machines with hundreds of barbed needles which moved in and out of loose wool fibres, locking and matting the fibres into a felt fabric. Barbed felting needles allow you to replicate this on a small scale at home for artwork.

To create a piece of needle felt, you tease out your wool fibres and place them over a dense foam pad. This gives your needle a base to work into, and it needs to be soft but strong enough to support your work. The felting needle is then moved in and out of the fibres in a straight motion until the fibres start to lock together. You need to make sure that you jab fairly deeply to ensure that you are felting the inner and base fibres and not just the top layers.

You can use any types of wool tops to needle felt. Coarser wools such as Welsh mountain are good for landscapes as they add texture, whereas softer wools such as merino and Bluefaced Leicester will give you a flat, smooth surface that is perfect for making flowers and leaves or for developing finer detail.

To shape, you can jab the needle in at a slight angle but care must be taken not to bend the needle. It is important to remember to turn the fibre shape frequently to ensure it does not stick to the foam pad.

If you intend to attach pieces together, leave some parts of the fibres fairly loose so that you can join pieces together more easily.

1

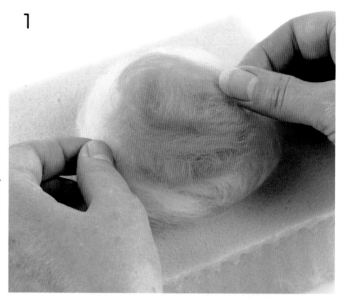

2

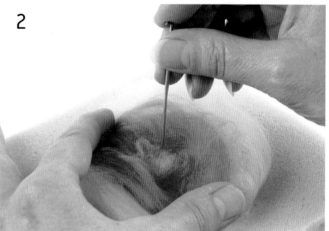

Needling

1 Tease some fibres out from your tops and roughly arrange them into a shape on your sponge block.

2 Using a 36 gauge barbed needle, tap it lightly in and out of the foam, straight through all of the fibres.

3 Continue working over the rest of the shape, needling in and out of the foam. Keep the needle straight, working in and out in the same direction to avoid breaking the needle.

3

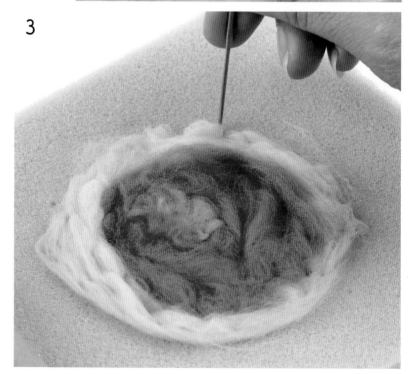

4

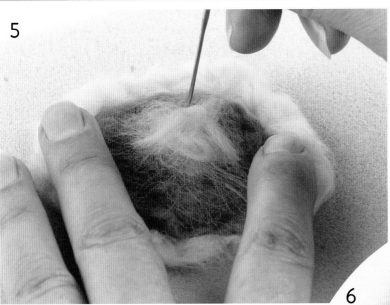

5

Finishing

4 Periodically lift the piece off the foam and place it back on. This is to avoid it becoming permanently attached as the fibres bind with the sponge. Use both hands as you lift the piece away, to help to maintain the shape.

5 As you work, the piece will begin to shrink a little as the fibres lock together. You can add more wool to alter the shape or pattern as you work; needling it into place alongside the rest.

6 Continue working until the piece has locked together into felt.

6

Free machine embroidery

Your sewing machine can be used to add decoration to your felt. I recommend using a darning foot on your machine but you can use a clear standard foot as shown here – or take it off completely! This enables you to see what you are creating more easily. Lengthening or shortening the stitch length, or using decorative stitches like zigzag stitch can create some interesting effects, too.

I typically use free machine embroidery for embellishment rather than structural purposes, so I use a variety of threads from specialised embroidery threads to regular buttonhole cotton. The type and colour of thread you use in your artwork is entirely up to you, and will depend on what results you want to achieve.

1

2

Setting up and precision work

1 Thread your machine with thread at the top and bottom. For simple outlining, put the feed dogs up and use a fairly long stitch length.

2 For sharp angles, leave the needle in the work, lift the foot and turn the piece.

3 Continue working round to the end.

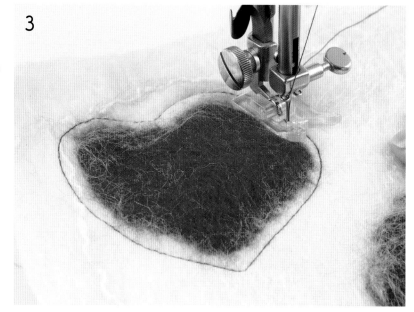

3

Looser work and finishing

4 For freer, looser work, change the stitch length and width to 0, and put the feed dogs down.

5 Leave the foot up, and then simply move the piece around while you 'doodle' with the machine. Use the machine like a paintbrush.

6 To finish, secure the threads by simply overstitching them, working back and forth over the same area.

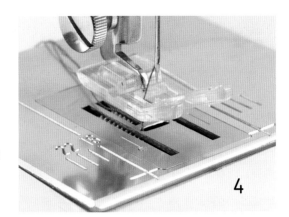

4

TIP: THE FOOT

If you prefer the reassurance of having the piece firmly in place, you can place the foot down. However, if your felt is thick, you may find that this hampers movement, which makes looser work much harder.
I recommend at least experimenting with the foot up, even if you do later decide to put it down.

5

6

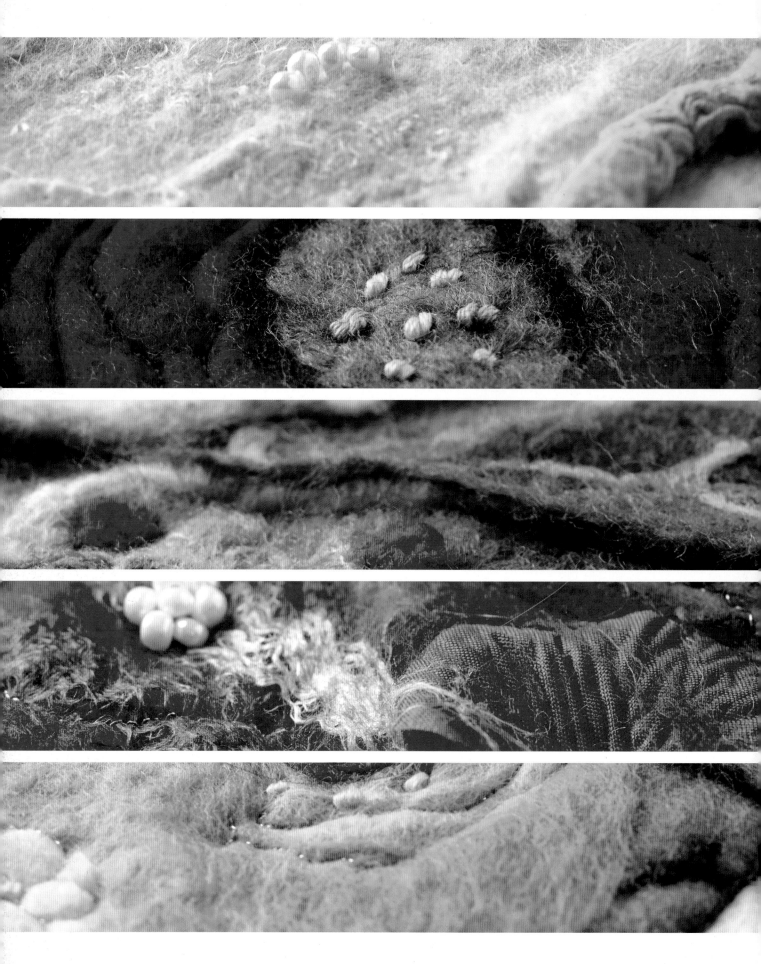

THE COLLECTIONS

In this part of the book, I invite you to explore five of my existing collections with me: *Water, Snow and Ice*; *Anne Boleyn*; *Abracadabra*; *Elizabeth Woodville*; and *Alice in Wonderland*. These are major themes that I have studied and developed in depth over many years; and for the projects in this book, I returned to my subject matter to explore the themes further. I reread my notes, visited new places, took more photographs, added more to my sketchbooks and tried out new ideas.

Following the step-by-step projects in each collection will allow you to produce felt artwork panels designed around the theme of the collection. Each panel demonstrates some of the felting techniques and materials explained earlier. The projects are accompanied by information on the process of refining initial inspiration into a solid design, in order to give you practical insight into this part of my artistic process.

Following each of the projects is a gallery of other artworks from the collection that were made in the same theme, to show you how far the techniques can be taken. I hope these serve as inspiration to you.

Each of the panels uses particular colours that relate to the themes. However, this is not prescriptive, and you may wish to choose to adapt the project using different colours or tones. As described in the section on colour (see pages 28–29), this is very much a personal choice. In fact, I would encourage you to make best use of your creativity – this is true not just for these projects but for your own work and artistic practice in general. Similarly, while I give suggested measurements for both the required materials and the expected outcome, you can decide whether to enlarge or decrease these to suit your own style and requirements.

How you display your finished panels is entirely up to you. You may like to add them to a sketchbook as a series of samples showing different techniques. You may like to frame the work to display it, or you may prefer to display the finished piece simply as a wall hanging. I sincerely hope that you enjoy making them as much as I have!

In this collection, I complement the beauty and power of the sea and swirls of fresh water with patterns created by ice forming, delicate snowflakes and blankets of snow. During my earliest research on this theme, I came to realise that the allure of water as a source of inspiration is irresistible. From trickling streams to ferocious waterfalls, from immense tropical oceans to the frozen landscapes of the Arctic, water is our planet's life force.

Step-by-step project: *Seascape*

Much of the inspiration for my *Water, Snow and Ice* collection is drawn from my father's love of sailing and our frequent trips to the coast when I was a child. As an adult I came to live in the Pennine hills, where I was struck by how quickly and unexpectedly the landscape could be transformed by water.

Taking this transformative power as more direct inspiration, I began trying to capture the effects of the water on the landscape in photographs and through sketches, painting and mixed media work. As my observations developed, I took to walking the hills and valleys around my home, crossing rivers and streams and watching with fascination the many cascading waterfalls that dot the countryside in the area. I then began to develop my ideas into samples and subsequently into the first works for this collection: three wearable art pieces entitled *Water*, *Snow* and *Ice*. These were followed quickly by a series of wall hangings, of which this step-by-step project is a continuation.

For this project, snow and ice are put on hold and we focus on water – the sea in particular. However, the theme in this collection remains open. You could easily adapt this project into a picture of snow-covered fields or a panorama of icy spears of grass moving upwards to cold, cloudy skies. You do not have to slavishly follow the letter of the instructions as written here!

This nuno felted panel depicts how the sea interacts with the land and the sky. Once you have finished, you might choose to frame the work with mounting card to give the work a feel of a painting. Equally, you might leave it unframed, so the edges of the work are visible.

'I am never so peaceful as when I am close to the sea. The salty wind in my face, the soft sand beneath my feet and the waves with their ruffles of white foam create a Heaven on earth!'

After the rain
Stream
in
West Yorkshire

Left by the tide
West Kirby
Wirral

Inspiration

Knowing that I wanted to put snow and ice to one side for this project, I felt it appropriate for the project to be based on the sea. This made it relatively easy to gather photographs and make sketches of coastal and beach scenes. I took trips to gather photographs from places such as the Holy Island of Lindisfarne, Criccieth in North Wales, and beaches in Scotland. I also looked in books and searched the internet for imagery relating to this theme.

Looking through the material I had gathered, I decided that a summer seascape would be the one to go for. It felt cheery and yet gave a sense of peace and tranquillity, while also offering an interesting variation on the theme that runs through the collection as a whole. Being moved and excited by what you are seeing will inevitably make your work more special and meaningful both to you and others.

With this idea in mind, I thought more on the relationship between the sea, the land and the sky. The three are often seen as individual entities, yet they merge together so beautifully – this provided the inspiration to create a piece which blends the three together into a single, cohesive artwork.

Design

To begin the practical process of turning ideas into reality, I experimented with acrylic and watercolour paints to produce quick sketches to evoke summer seas, stormy seas, waves, cloud formations and light. I went on to develop these sketches and paintings into textile samples using different fabrics, colour ways and mixed media, in order to see how best to translate the colours into felt and fabric. Some of them can be seen on these pages.

Felting techniques

Nuno felting stood out for me as the natural choice for this piece of work because of the natural textures that are created during the making process. It also seems to have a kinetic energy about it which reflects and represents how the sea constantly moves. This technique was thus a natural fit for the panel as a whole.

To correctly bring my inspiration into reality, I wanted to infuse the work with a light feeling. To achieve this, the wool fibres and other media utilised within the project were layered very finely to keep the work delicate. I experimented with teasing the fibres out freely and gently so that they maintained a sense of movement yet remain defined. This worked well, so I practised on a few pieces before launching into the main project.

Colour palette

As water is the central theme of the collection as a whole, I decided on the colours for the sea section first, then chose colours that complemented it for the sky and sand pieces. For the sky, I selected coloured merino wool tops that had a summer feel: sky blue, aquamarine and white. White merino was chosen to give the effect of white fluffy clouds in the sky, while hints of pale pink and lilac mulberry silks and heat-fusible iridescent fibres helped to suggest a summer's day. For the sand, I selected creams with hints of brown, knitting wools and mulberry silks creating texture, with sunlight depicted through the use of sparkly heat-fusible iridescent fibres.

The samples I worked on cotton muslin seemed to work best for this particular project, and I was especially pleased with those in which I had hand-dyed the fabric myself. The use of natural cotton muslin for all three pieces helps to link the pieces together, and also plays on the idea of the natural world: natural fabrics with the seascape itself. The fabrics were coloured using cold water dyes using the earlier sketches to suggest a colour palette, going from a darker aquamarine-tinged turquoise to represent the sea and a more pale turquoise for the summer sky.

Challenges

Having decided to make a panel made up of three individual pieces, I needed to decide how to combine them into a cohesive whole. To achieve this, I incorporated silks, beads and heat-fusible iridescent fibres into all three sections of the feltwork. These add common colours and textures that help to combine the three pieces into one artwork, variously representing the shimmer of sunlight on moving water and the shine of shallow pools of seawater on the sand.

Physically, the pieces were delicately hand stitched together using a simple straight stitch, leaving the organic edge of the nuno felt exposed. This adds to the overall texture and definition of the work and helps the three pieces to work together.

Key guidelines

- Create smaller samples to ensure the chosen fabric is suitable for purpose before embarking on a large nuno felt project like this.

- Use wispy fibres and avoid clumps, which are much harder to engage with the fabric and tend to lock onto themselves instead.

- Always rinse your fabric before use. This will extract any dressing or chemicals that still remain from the manufacturing process.

- Use merino wool as coarser wools will be harder to felt.

- Use only tepid/lukewarm water until fibres appear on the reverse of your work.

- Use natural cloth only. Closely-woven or synthetic fabrics will usually end with the wool fibres locking onto one another rather than the selected fabric. Cotton muslin, scrim or silk chiffon all work well.

- Cover silk and other non-felting fibres with slivers of merino wool tops to lock them onto the fabric.

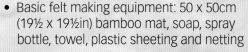

WHAT YOU NEED

- Basic felt making equipment: 50 x 50cm (19½ x 19½in) bamboo mat, soap, spray bottle, towel, plastic sheeting and netting
- Merino wool tops: white, cream, aquamarine, sky blue, light brown and fawn
- Knitting wools: sand-coloured poodle wool and cream mohair
- Mulberry silks: white, cream and variegated (lilac and pink)
- Heat-fusible iridescent fibres: lilac and purple
- Natural cotton muslin: three 35 x 20cm (14 x 8in) pieces
- Fabric dye: turquoise and aquamarine
- Embroidery needle and white cotton thread
- Pearl and sand-coloured beads
- Embroidery scissors
- Felting needle and pad

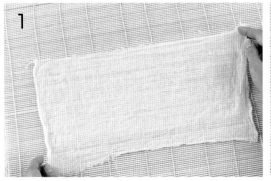

Sand: laying out the wool

1 Lay plastic sheet with a towel on top to protect your table surface, then place a 35 x 20cm (14 x 8in) piece of natural cotton muslin on top of your rolling mat. Make sure the muslin has been washed to remove any chemical dressing left from the fabric's manufacture.

2 Cover the whole surface with a fine layer of cream merino tops, with the fibres running from right to left. Overlay the edges as shown with the fibres, as this will help prevent a raw edge later on.

3 Using fawn merino tops, tease out some more fibres and lay a few touches here and there across the surface, again with the fibres running horizontally.

4 Repeat the process, adding a few touches with the light brown and fawn variegated merino tops, a few touches of the mulberry silk, and a few strands of the knitting wool. Overlay them in turn, and make sure they all run horizontally.

5 Lay a few fine strands of the cream merino tops over the surface. This will help lock the silk and synthetic strands in place when you felt it.

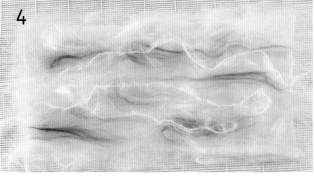

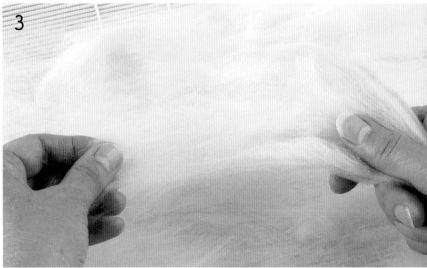

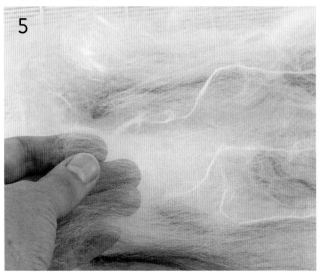

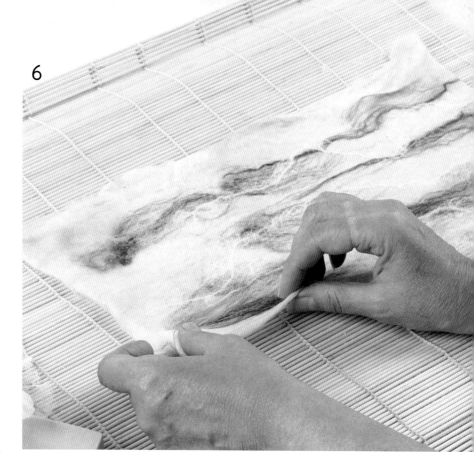

6

Sand: nuno felting

6 Following the instructions on pages 34–37, nuno felt the piece together. When you remove the netting, fold the overlapping fibres under the edges.

7 Continue nuno felting the piece. You are aiming to emphasise the horizontal creases and details in the beach, so do not turn the piece as you work. Once the fibres have bonded, you can pick the piece up in your hands to continue felting it (see inset). Continue working until the piece measures roughly 30 x 12cm (11¾ x 4¾in).

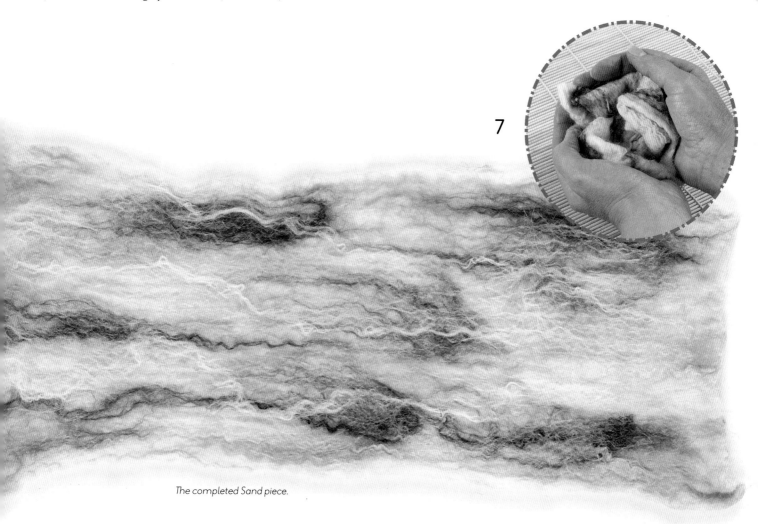

7

The completed Sand piece.

Sea: laying out the wool

8 Put the sand piece to one side. Following the manufacturer's instructions, dye one of the pieces of cotton muslin aquamarine. Lie it on top of your rolling mat. Cover the whole surface with a fine layer of aquamarine merino tops, with the fibres running from right to left, as before. Again, overlay the edges of the muslin with the fibres.

9 As before, add some variation to the surface by adding a few touches of sky blue merino tops, cream merino tops, cream mohair decorative yarn, variegated lilac and purple and white mulberry silks, and lilac iridescent fibres on top. As before, make sure they all are arranged loosely horizontally; but you can add the suggestion of waves at this point, if you wish.

10 Lay a few loose touches of natural merino wool over the surface to help the fabrics felt together, then lay the netting over the top, ensuring it overlays it completely.

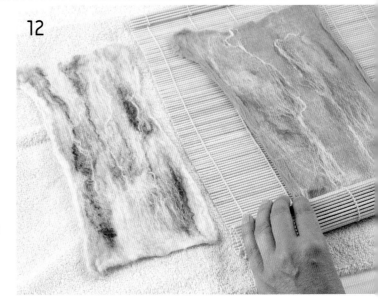

Sea: nuno felting

11 Wet the piece with tepid water and begin to nuno felt the piece. Tuck the edges under when you remove the netting.

12 Continue nuno felting the sea piece. As it begins to felt and tighten, take it out and compare it to the beach piece in size. If it is looking like it will end up too wide, turn the piece through ninety degrees and felt it until it shortens a little. If the piece looks like it will shrink to near the correct size anyway, turning it is not necessary.

13 Once the piece is felting fairly tightly, you can pick it up in your hands and felt it there to work more quickly.

14 Compare the sea piece in size to the beach piece. If it is correct – roughly 30 x 12cm (11¾ x 4¾in) – you have finished. Otherwise, you can stretch it slightly or continue felting.

13

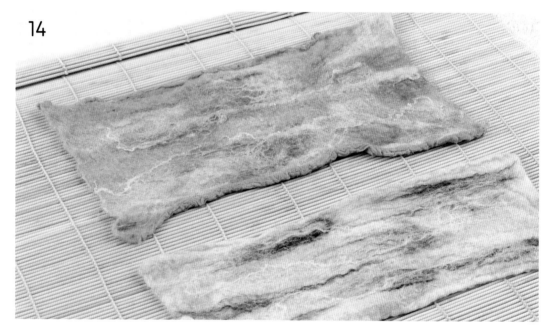

14

The completed Sea piece.

Sky: laying out the wool and nuno felting

15 Following the manufacturer's instructions, dye one of the pieces of cotton muslin pale turquoise. Lie it on your rolling mat. Cover the surface, overlaying the edges, with a fine horizontal layer of pure white merino tops. Add some touches across the piece using small amounts of sky blue merino tops, variegated lilac and purple and white mulberry silks. Add some slightly thicker pieces of pure white merino tops as clouds, then use some fine wisps of pure white merino to overlay and help secure the silks.

16 Lay the netting over the top as before, then begin the nuno felting technique by using the spray bottle to wet the whole area with tepid water.

17 Roll the piece, then unroll it and peel away the netting. Fold the fibres under the edges and rewet the edges.

18 Continue nuno felting as for the beach and sea pieces until the sky piece is roughly the same size: 30 x 12cm (11¾ x 4¾in).

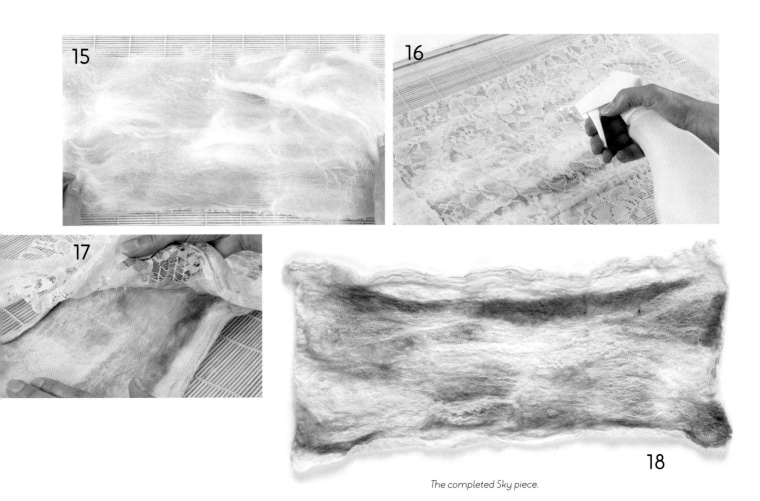

The completed Sky piece.

Embellishing: beads on the sand piece

19 Rinse the pieces to remove any remaining soap, then lay them on a flat surface overlapping one another, as shown, to dry naturally.

20 To evoke the glistening wet sand, use a needle and white or complementary thread to attach some sparkly sand-coloured beads on the beach piece. Secure the beads in place on the back with a double stitch (see inset).

21 Sew the beads on in roughly horizontal lines, to harmonise with the horizontal shapes already on the piece that were created through the felting process. Keep the groups near the bottom of the piece to help create a sense of distance.

22 Add two or three lines of beads in total. Remember that sometimes less is more – you are trying to create the impression of sunlight on shallow pools left by the ebbing tide, not to overload your feltwork by covering it with beads.

19

20

21
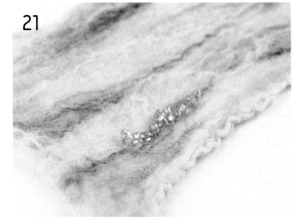

22
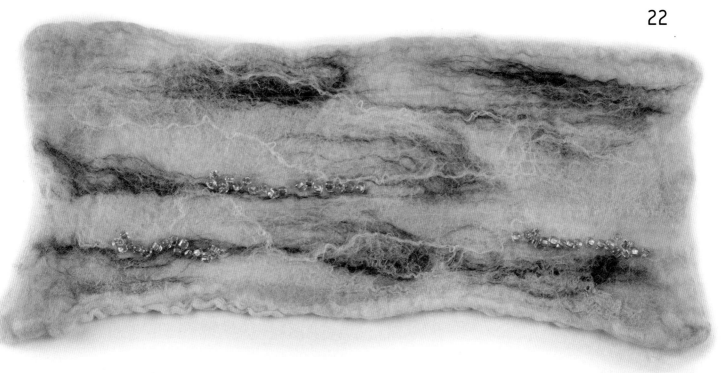

Embellishing: beads on the sea piece

23 Find a light-coloured and horizontal wavy line on the sea piece, and sew on pearl beads to accentuate it, again using the sewing needle and white thread.

24 Sew the beads on in horizontal groups towards the bottom of the sea piece, in the same way as for the sand piece.

Embellishing: needle felting on the sky piece

25 Tease off a short length – approximately 7.5cm (3in) – of black merino wool and twist it between your fingers to help lock the threads together a little.

26 Place the sky piece over your needle felting pad and place the black wool on top, loosely into the shape of a 'V' to represent a silhouetted gull.

27 Following the instructions on pages 38–39, needle felt the gull in place. Start in the fold of the 'V', so the centre is secured first. This will help you to keep the shape as you work.

28 Work until the gull is felted into place, then add another in the same way.

Assembly and finishing

29 Pin the pieces together, making sure that the beach piece is beneath the sea piece, with the edge of the sea overlapping the sand. This creates the impression of a small wave coming up onto the beach. Overlap the bottom edge of the sky piece over the top of the sea piece to create a more natural-looking horizon.

30 Using white cotton thread, stitch along the pinned edges on the reverse of the work. Do not work all the way through the pieces of felt; instead, work into them and out to the overlapping edge. This hides the stitches on the front of the work and finishes the piece. The completed artwork is shown overleaf.

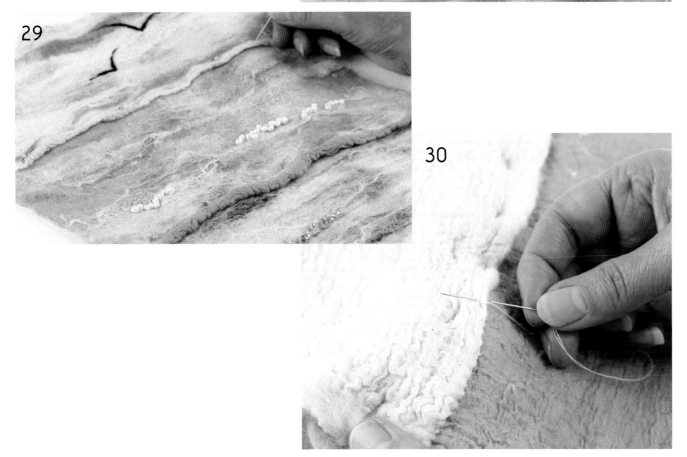

The finished piece

Incorporating nuno felt making alongside beading, needle felting and simple hand embroidery, this piece combines some relatively simple techniques into a more complex finished artwork.

Here I have focussed on the 'water' aspect of the *Water, Snow and Ice* collection, to the exclusion of the other aspects. This demonstrates that the theme of your collection can be as restrictive or loose as you wish. Sometimes having tight design constraints – such as limiting yourself to an aspect of a broader theme – can help to generate imaginative ideas, while at other times having few or no limits – by merely hinting at other works – can be liberating.

Detail of intersection

This shows where the sea overlaps the sand – the ridge created where the two pieces are stitched together suggests a small wave which echoes the watery feel. The sand-coloured beads create texture and light.

Detail of pearl beads

Here the pearl beads represent sea foam and waves cresting – so they are restricted to the bottom half of the sea piece to suggest they are nearer to us.

Detail of needle felted gulls

The silhouetted gulls – created using needle felting – add a point of interest to the sky.

Shades of Blue

The sixth, and to date final, dress/costume in the *Water, Snow and Ice* collection, *Shades of Blue* shares a common theme with *Seascape*, the project panel in this book: the theme of water. Both were inspired by my frequent walks along the banks of gushing rivers and trickling streams, and also along the coast, but where *Seascape* focussed on the sea, this piece takes a more symbolic direction and represents the allure of water as our precious life source.

Different shades of blue and white were used to depict changes in light on the water's surface as well as changes of depth. It is longer at the back to illustrate the flowing and continuous nature of waters such as these. It combines variegated dyed cotton muslin, merino wool tops in different shades of blue, white and cream, mulberry silks and various types of knitting wool, both natural and synthetic, to add texture and interest.

Like *Seascape*, it was worked in separate sections of nuno felt that were later combined to give a wonderful draping quality and soft texture to the finished dress.

Detail of back

Satin ribbons in coordinating shades of purple, blue and white are used to tie up the back of the dress. They are left long and free flowing to emphasise the movement of water.

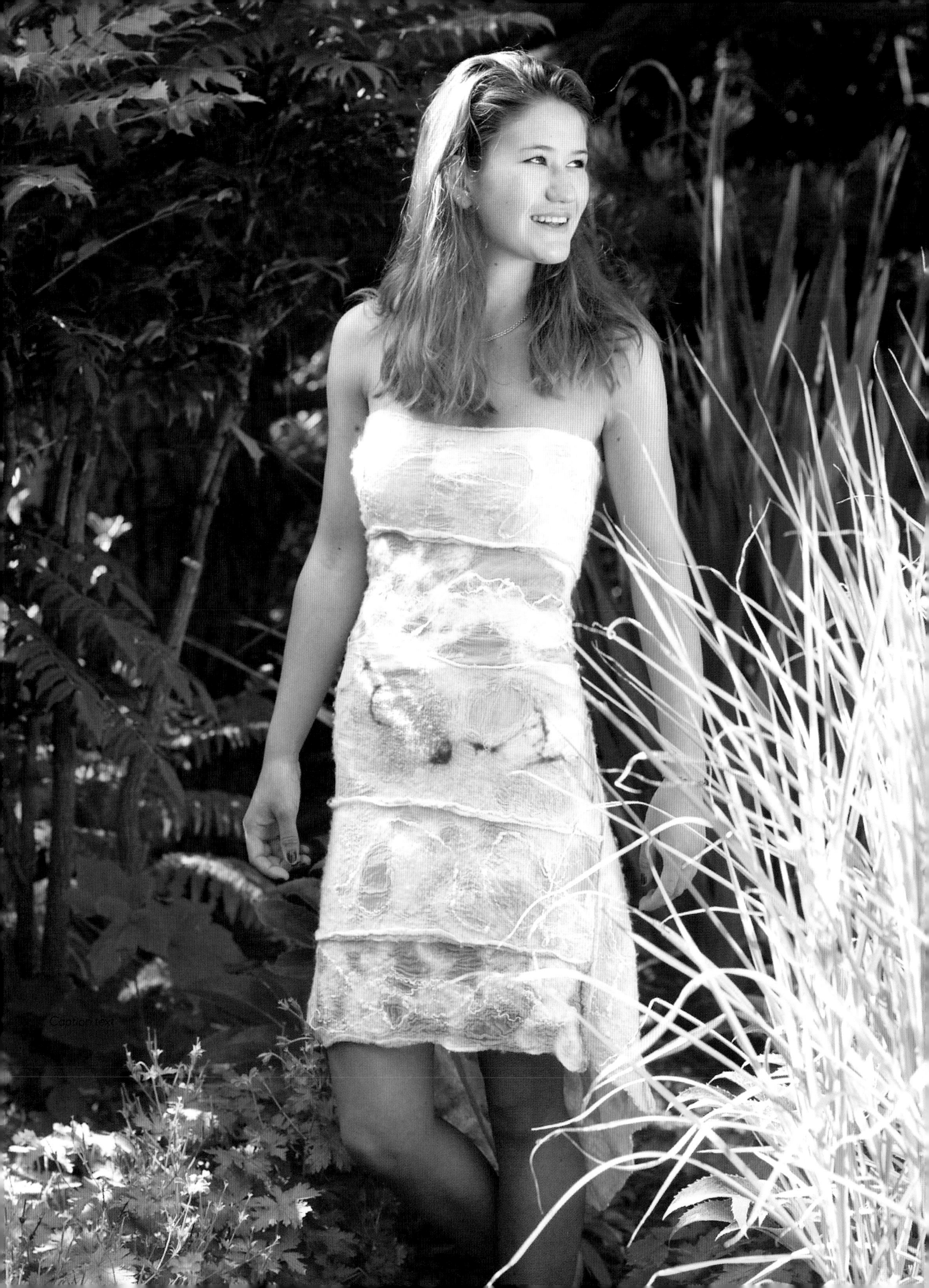

A Walk on the Beach

I am always fascinated by the powerful rise and fall of the tide, where one minute you can be looking at a vast stretch of sand, the next minute it is covered by water. And the 'treasures' that the tide leaves behind – amazing! This evokes for me those moments – different each time – when I have found myself on the seashore admiring the transient seaweed, crustaceans, pebbles, sea foam and shallow water pools. I never tire of these superficially similar, yet unique in detail, moments, and this piece encapsulates that impression for me.

This large nuno felted wall hanging takes as its inspiration the simple idea of 'sand on the beach'. It was an important part of the inspiration for *Seascape*, which illustrates how one idea can lead to another. Utilising the nuno felting technique, just like the project, *A Walk on the Beach* was created using a double layer of cream silk chiffon encapsulating raffia, scraps of velvet, braid, synthetic and natural wool – including, of course, merino wool. Compare this piece to the sand section of *Seascape* to see the similarities and differences.

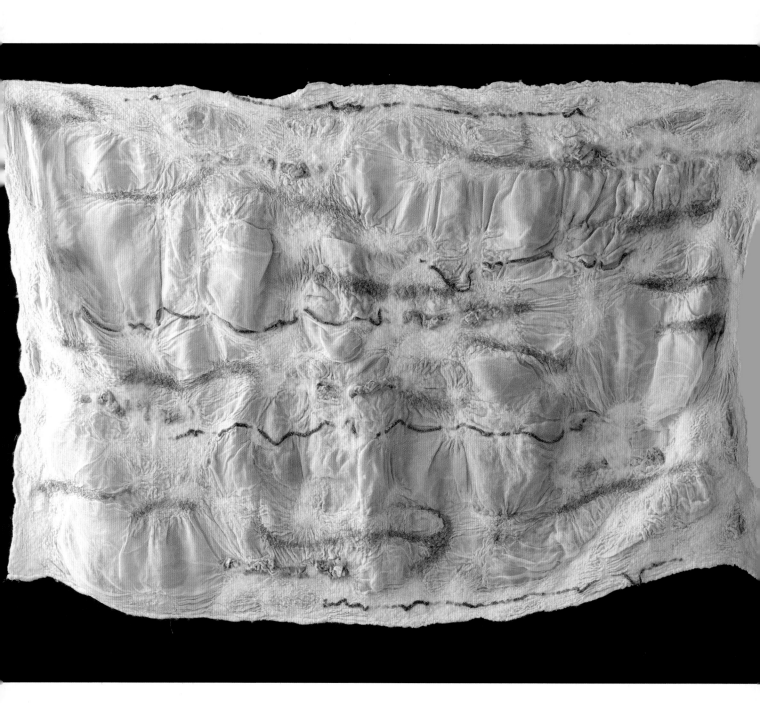

Detail of velvet element

This detail shows a close-up of velvet fabric incorporated into the panel. Distressed and scrunched by the process of nuno felting, I have used the velvet to help create a visual representation of the broken shells and crustaceans scattered about the beach. Merino wool slivers were used to hold the fabric in place, adding texture and bringing the piece to life.

Anne Boleyn

As a child growing up, I was always fascinated by ancient castles and historical places of interest. More so, I wondered at the people who had once lived there, imagining the sound of their footsteps on the cobbles and spiral staircases for example, and their whispers in darkened corners. One figure in particular seemed to haunt my imagination: a woman called Anne Boleyn.

Anne's exact date of birth is unrecorded, although historians believe it was around 1502 or 1503. She was probably born at either Hever Castle in Kent or Blickling Hall in Norfolk. What we do know is that King Henry VIII of England was infatuated by her and in 1533 they were married, with Anne becoming queen. Anne gradually fell from favour with Henry, and she was eventually arrested and imprisoned in the Tower of London on charges of high treason. She met a gruesome end: beheaded on the scaffold on the 19th of May 1536.

Step-by-step project: *A Fallen Rose*

My fascination with Anne led to my first collection of costumes. The core of the *Anne Boleyn* collection is ten costumes of wearable art that each relate to the events that shaped Anne's life – in particular those that led to her execution.

The panel on the following pages takes some inspiration from the Tudor rose, symbol of King Henry's royal dynasty, into which Anne married. I have kept this project relatively simple – strong use of colour means the design will be more successful as long as you can resist the temptation to overwork it. Sometimes – indeed often – less is more!

'As a small child visiting ancient castles and places, I often wondered who had once lived there – and imagined their faces hidden in dark shadows and their footsteps faintly heard upon the cobblestones.'

Inspiration

You will have gathered that Anne Boleyn is something of a passion of mine. Why I feel this way about a woman who lived almost five hundred years ago and who is often written about in a derogatory way, I am not completely sure. However, I do know that as my childhood intuition developed into more adult critical enquiry, I began to see that much of the source material available about Anne Boleyn is both inconsistent and contradictory. The injustices ranged against her have fuelled my passion, and will hopefully ignite yours too!

During my research into the world of Anne Boleyn, I came across one of my favourite portraits of this queen of England – one in which she holds a single red rose, the symbol of the House of Lancaster. This led to thoughts of the Tudor rose, which combines the white rose of the House of York with the red rose of the House of Lancaster, and which appears frequently in books, portraits, architecture, historical documents and other material associated with the Tudors. In addition, the rose has many traditional associations when viewed simply as a flower, amongst them femininity, passion and excitement, all of which are very appropriate to Anne's story.

Wanting a strong central image that symbolised Anne, my first ideas revolved around her initials. In pursuing this, I created a number of small samples initially concentrating on the letter 'A'. I practised working in free machine embroidery and also needle felting the letter. I was not completely convinced by these results, and it was around about this time that I came across the aforementioned portrait of Anne holding a red rose. While I had seen the portrait before, this time it created what I can only describe as a rush of excitement in me – I realised immediately that I wanted to create a panel with the strong image of a rose as the focus.

The samples shown on these pages were made by colouring paper with vibrant red and black acrylic paint – both splashing it from a brush as well as mono printing. I then tore and overlaid the painted papers, added scrunched and knotted tissue paper, and worked over the results with free machine embroidery. I began to use zigzag stitch and black thread to communicate the feelings of violence, darkness and containment and evoke the sharp edge of the executioner's sword before it slashed into – to use her own words – Anne's 'little neck'.

This shows how inspiration and design can feed into one another – do not be afraid to return to an earlier stage if you feel your artwork will benefit. My experimental work using paints, paper and imagery, as seen on these pages, helps me to create a mood and invoke my own emotions in relation to the work as it progresses. Very often just the physicality of tearing papers and splashing paint onto a blank page or canvas can bring together my thoughts and feelings on the subject matter. Mining a well of inspiration can be as physical and practical as the later, more considered, design work.

Design

Techniques

In the *Anne Boleyn* collection, both the first costume, entitled *Desire* (this can be seen on pages 82–83), and the final costume, *Charade*, were made using the wet felting technique. It seemed an obvious choice to make this panel using the same techniques, so I practised the wet felting method utilising merino wool tops and mulberry silks for the basis. As explained later, I decided to add embellishments using both free machine and hand embroidery later in the design process.

Colour palette

For this collection I utilised a limited colour palette of mainly black and red; I felt it appropriate for this project to continue in the same way. I also used green and yellow in small quantities to add interest and highlights to lift the work. It was important to add the green, because the green stalk and a tiny leaf within the inspirational portrait can be clearly seen. I also included a touch of purple – this is significant and appropriate here because it relates to nobility and royalty.

Development

My research on the Tudors brought carved bedsteads, wooden furniture panels and embroidered hangings from the period that were all rectangular. My initial design samples echoed this shape, but after producing some practice pieces, I decided instead to change to a square format. This still links to several carved ceilings and bedsteads I have seen from the period, but it complemented the arrangement of roses I wanted to use much better.

Happy with the shape of the project, I then practised a variety of designs incorporating the leaves and stalk alongside the rose flower. Although happy with how the design had evolved, I felt that the felt alone was somewhat flat and needed a lift. This is the point when I decided to add mulberry silks and embroidery to my sampling. This embellishment added enough sheen to the design for me to rest happily and allow me to start the final piece.

WHAT YOU NEED

- Basic felt making equipment: 50 x 50cm (19½ x 19½in) bamboo mat, soap, spray bottle, towel, plastic sheeting, and netting
- Merino wool tops: black, red, yellow-green and cool green
- Mulberry silks: variegated pink, variegated lilac, variegated purple
- Sewing machine
- Machine embroidery thread: red and green
- Embroidery needle and yellow and green thread
- Embroidery scissors
- Plastic carrier bag

Key guidelines

- Stick to a limited colour palette – a strong subject matter such as this requires you not to be tempted to use any colours outside your initial planned range.

- Continuously turn your work during the felt making process. This prevents shrinkage in one direction only – which will result in your design being distorted or lost completely.

- Keep fibres wispy to encourage them to lock onto your base layer of wool.

- Remember to lightly cover mulberry silks with wispy merino slivers to help bond them to the base fibres.

- If a particular area is not attaching as well as others, concentrate on this area until it is firmly fixed before continuing. Cover it with the net, add more soap and water and rub in a circular motion.

Laying out the wool

1 Protect your surface by putting a towel on top of plastic sheet. Draw out black merino tops and lay out a layer on your rolling mat in a rectangle measuring 36 x 33.5cm (14¼ x 13¼in). Make sure all the fibres run from top to bottom.

2 Lay out another layer of black merino wool on top. This time, lay the wool on at a right angle to the previous layer, so that the fibres all run from left to right.

3 Lay a third layer on top, again at right angles to the one beneath – so the fibres run from top to bottom on this third layer.

Adding roses

4 Pull off a fair amount of red merino tops and shape them into a rough circle to represent a red rose. The size of the rose is not critical; but you will need to decide how many you wish to add and adjust the size you make them. Here, each measures approximately 10cm (4in) in diameter.

5 Place the rose on top of the black rectangle. Make and place a few more, to fill between a third and a half of the surface.

TIP: ADAPT

Be free with your design and enjoy the flow of your work. Do not get too hung up about a prescriptive number of roses or leaves.

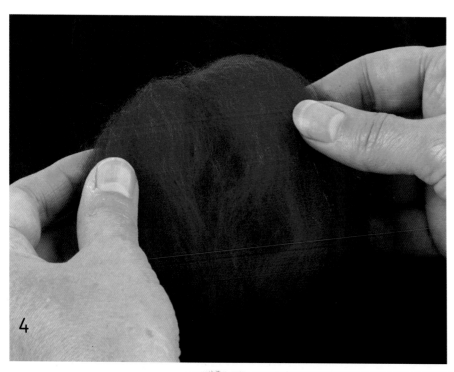

4

5

Detailing the roses

6 Draw off small amounts of yellow-green merino tops, shape them into circles and place one in the centre of each rose.

7 Add smaller amounts of cool green to the centre of each rose in the same way.

8 Tease out tiny amounts of black merino tops, twist them between your fingers to make wisps of wool (see inset), then add one or two to each rose to add texture and interest.

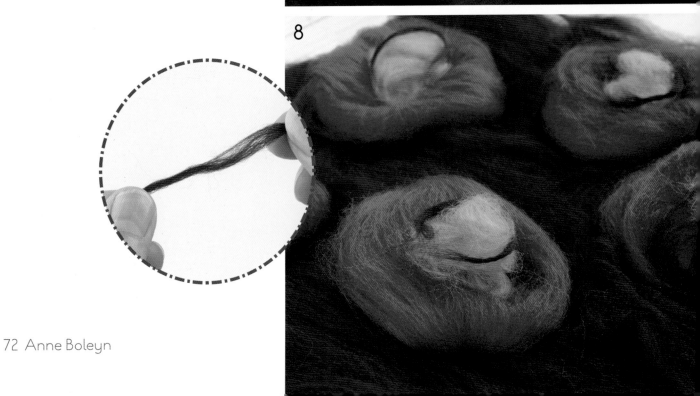

Adding leaves and a border

9 Draw larger amounts of yellow-green merino tops, twist the ends together and open out the centres to make leaf shapes. Place a few around the roses to fill a little of the background.

10 Tease out tiny amounts of cool green merino tops and make wisps to add veins and other detailing to the leaves.

11 Using pink-purple variegated mulberry silks, create a fine, broken border around the edges of the picture. Add some tiny touches of the same mulberry silk amongst the leaves and roses, and cover these touches lightly using small wisps of merino wool.

9

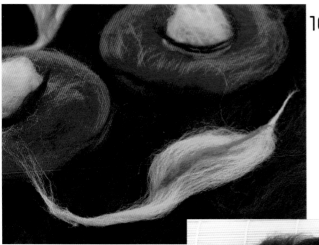

10

11

Felting the piece

12 Lay a large piece of netting over the whole piece and use the spray bottle to spray hot water over the whole piece. The addition of the roses and other details means that the wool is very thick, so it is important that it is thoroughly wetted to avoid dry areas remaining inside, which will prevent it felting properly.

13 Use your hands to smooth the piece down and ensure the water is spread throughout. If any areas feel slightly fluffy, that area is still dry; so add more water with the spray bottle.

14 Once you are happy the wool is properly wetted, draw the soap over the whole piece.

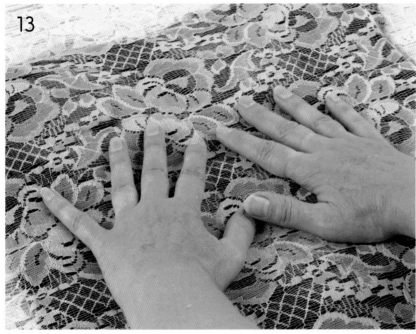

15 Working especially carefully to ensure all the layers and details stay in place, roll the mat up tightly.

16 Place the palms of your hands on top of the rolled-up mat and rub back and forth vigorously around a hundred times to start felting the piece. Unroll the mat and check that all the pieces have remained in position.

17 Carefully remove the netting, lift the piece away from the mat, turn it through ninety degrees and place it back on the mat.

TIP: WETTING THICKER WOOL

To ensure thicker pieces – like the one in this project – are properly wetted, you can turn them over once they have started to felt together (i.e. after the first rolling) and wet the back.

15

16

17

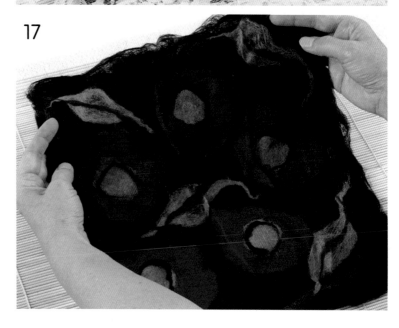

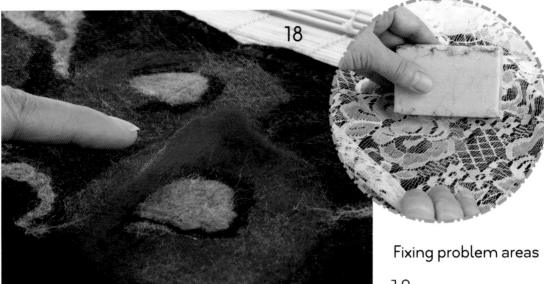

Fixing problem areas

18 Continue wet felting the piece following the instructions on pages 30–33. If any areas are revealed to have lifted away (main picture), press them back down into place, lay the net back over the top and add more soap, as shown in the inset.

19 Next, rub the area vigorously with a scrunched-up plastic bag. This forces the wet soapy water down into the area and felts the fibres.

20 Lift the netting away to check the piece has felted properly. If it has not, then repeat the steps above until it is secured.

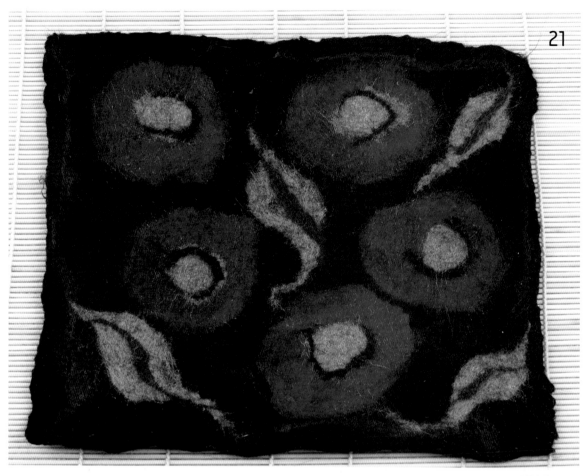

21

22

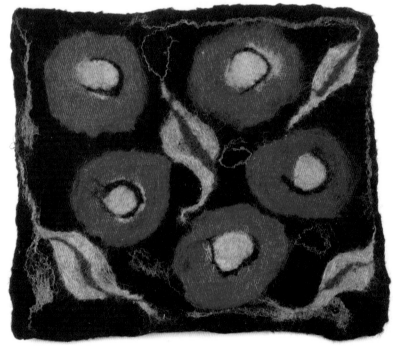

23

21 Continue wet felting the piece, remembering to turn the piece each time; until the piece measures approximately 28 x 25.5cm (11 x 10in).

22 Rinse the piece in clean water and wring it out to remove excess water and soap.

23 Pull the piece back into shape and leave it to dry naturally.

Embellishing: free machine embroidery

24 Thread up the top and bottom of your sewing machine with red embroidery thread. Following the free machine embroidery instructions on pages 40–41, begin to embroider loose wavy spirals on one of the roses, in order to suggest the shape of petals.

25 Work from the inside of the flower outwards to the edges in a loose spiral. Keep the red thread within the red felted area; do not go onto the black.

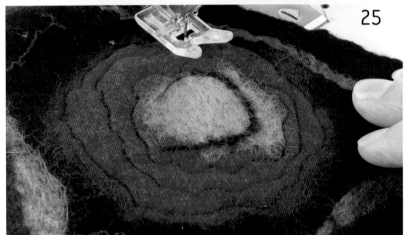

26 Secure the thread by overstitching, then trim any loose ends with embroidery scissors and embroider the other roses in the same way.

27 Thread your sewing machine with green embroidery thread in both the top and bottom, and use free machine embroidery to add some detail to the leaves: work up the middle of the vein (see inset) then add some freehand smaller offshoot veins on each leaf. Oversew the threads to secure and trim any excess.

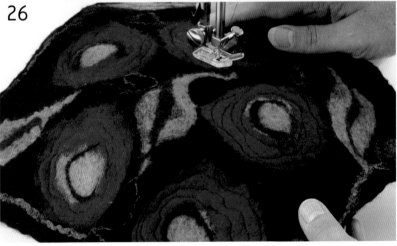

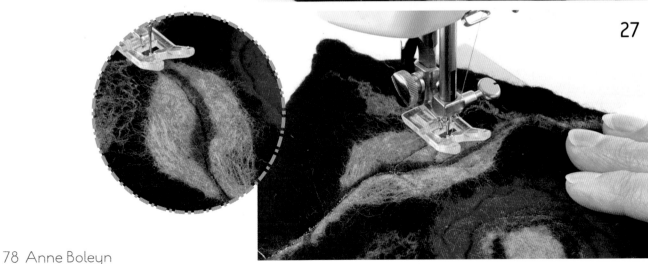

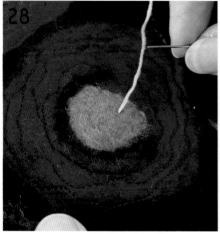

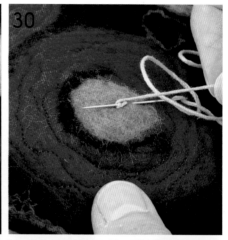

Embellishing: French knots

28 Thread a large-eyed needle with a short length of yellow cotton thread, tie a knot in the end and pull the thread through from the back in the centre of one of the roses.

29 Take the needle in and back out just next to where you brought it through, as shown.

30 Wrap the thread round the emerging end of the needle twice.

31 Hold the wrapped thread in place and draw through.

32 Take the needle back down very close to the knot, draw through and secure to finish the French knot. Trim any excess thread.

33 Add more French knots in the centre of each of the roses. Add as many or as few as you wish, and add some variety and interest with green thread. Secure the thread and trim to finish. The completed artwork is shown overleaf.

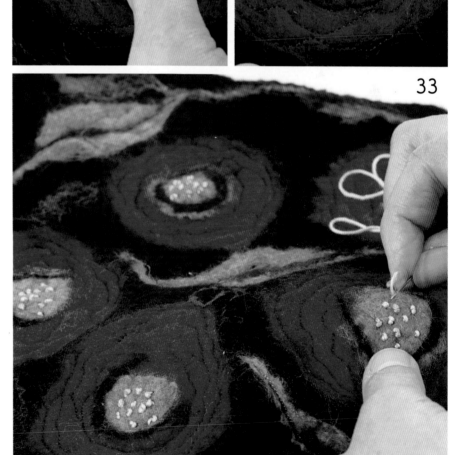

The finished piece

Part of my work on Anne Boleyn is my attempt – however small – to set the record straight on her life. This piece hopes to remind people to read between the lines of the accounts we have of her life, and bear in mind the many and varied political agendas of the times before coming to a personal judgement on the queen.

Creating a piece of felt with a distinct, detailed design like this requires careful felting, but the rewards of achieving a strong image that keeps the colours strongly separated are well worth the effort.

Note how the wisps of wool hold the mulberry silks in place without obscuring them, and how the embroidery – both that added with the machine and that added by hand – adds detail and gives a lift to the focal areas of the roses.

Details of *A Fallen Rose*

These details of the finished piece show how using a simple running stitch on your sewing machine can add definition and a three-dimensional quality to felt. It also highlights how much the work is brought to life by such details. The thread brings a crucial quality to this project: giving the sense that although Anne is no longer with us, in history she lives on. It also creates the sense of leaves floating on a stream or blowing in the wind, in search of a place of rest, so rebirth can begin.

Here I have used black thread on the red roses, and green machine embroidery thread to add veins to the leaves. In addition, French knots were added in yellow hand embroidery thread in the centres of the roses.

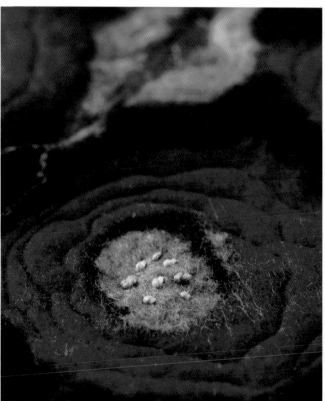

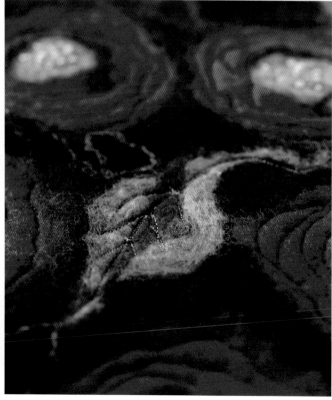

Desire

The *Anne Boleyn* collection contains ten wearable art pieces. *Desire* is the first. It represents Henry and Anne's early courtship, in particular the King's ever-growing desire for Anne. The technique of felt making seemed appropriate – I imagined Henry and Anne's love for one another developing, sensual and soft, like the laying out of the fibres, leading on to the robust locking together of the fibres, the violence of what was to come.

The piece also symbolises my idea of the beginning of the end for Anne. Red and black merino wool tops, chosen to create a painterly effect, represent blood, loss and death. The red and black fibres blend together easily, seamlessly and to good effect.

Wanting to suggest nobility and aristocracy, I incorporated slashes in the design using a black chiffon fabric. Slashes were a fashion statement during the Tudor period – intended to reveal the opulence of further layers of clothing beneath – and there are many paintings of Henry wearing this fashionable clothing, from which I drew my inspiration.

Desire uses similar techniques as *A Fallen Rose*. I used free machine embroidery, hand embroidery and felt making. Both pieces use a limited colour palette as well as symbols of the Tudor period, such as slashes and red roses.

Opposite:

Desire

For me, it is essential that my wearable art pieces are actually worn, as shown to the right. I feel it brings the work to life, adding movement and context.

Below:

Close-up detail of *Desire*

This image shows some of the free machine embroidery and hand embroidery around the slashes. The machine embroidery was worked using black thread and a zigzag stitch to suggest the violence and suddenness of Anne's forthcoming demise. Large raised stitches using hand embroidery thread visualise my ideas of Anne's impending imprisonment within the Tower of London.

Possession

The second of ten wearable art pieces in the *Anne Boleyn* collection, *Possession* is worked in a way to portray leaves and vines. This costume is intended to suggest the forces beginning to wrap around Anne, choking her with 'ownership' and a position from which there was no escape.

Made with a variegated pearlised thread in shades of red, it utilises hundreds of metres of free machine embroidery. As with *Desire* (see pages 82–83), I used black organza fabric, limiting my colour choices. Some of the leaves include the use of hand-rolled felt which has been cut to shape and size and stitched to the work.

Like the project panel, *Possession* includes the use of leaves to link it both to the main body of work and also to the images of the Tudor rose, the crown and its possession of Anne in a time of extreme political gamesmanship.

Detail of *Possession*

The use of satin stitch is shown clearly here. Note the complexity of the leaves and tendrils as they intertwine, gradually closing in around Anne and suffocating the very life out of her.

Abracadabra

I have always loved fairies, whether in artwork like Cicely Mary Baker's beautiful illustrations, in literature such as Tinkerbell in J. M. Barrie's *Peter Pan*, or simply in the imagination, like the famous photographs of the Cottingley fairies, staged not so far from where I live. I find the idea of fairies using their magical power for good deeds attractive. I think they are fascinating, with their appearance of tiny beautiful winged humans and their mysterious nature, visible to only a privileged few.

Fairies provided a great source of inspiration for me for the *Abracadabra* collection because of their magical ability to transform bad into good, sad into happy, and to help humans live their dreams: 'Cinderella, you shall go to the ball!' A magic wand is waved and – abracadabra – life is magically transformed into something else!

This collection consists mainly of pieces made up from pieces of older artworks, changed and combined into beautiful new forms. It could so easily have been entitled *Construct, Deconstruct, Reconstruct*, in that pieces of work from two of my other collections, *Haunting* and *Brontë* were taken apart and remade. With scissors in hand, I began to look through some of pieces from these collections and selected a few. Without hesitation, I began to cut them up, then reconstruct them through layering, overlaying, and mixing old fragments with completely new pieces.

There are currently twelve costumes in the *Abracadabra* collection, with a few ideas still in their embryonic stages. Part of the appeal of the collection is the way that old ideas can be recycled, reframed and renewed – with results that are far more diverse than some of my other, more tightly focussed collections. As a result, there are a number of disparate themes that suffuse the collection, including woodland and the glow of moonlight. Unlike my other collections, *Abracadabra* is influenced by my thoughts and ideas at a given moment and, as such, offers me the freedom to dip in out of it as I wish – quite fittingly for a series themed around magic!

Step-by-step project: *Woodland Berries*

The theme of woodland forms the basis of this project. By following the step-by-step instructions, you will be able to create a nuno felted panel resembling bark on a tree, together with needle felted leaves and red berries.

'I imagined fairies in the woodland ready for a feast of magical delight; moon haze, dew drops and tiny dancing feet...'

'Seasonal changes fascinate me – spring's new growth, the vibrant colours and shades of summer and the fall of leaves in autumn all speak to me with a magic in their collective voice. Abracadabra...'

Inspiration

I am fortunate enough to live in the countryside surrounded by trees, fields and streams. Many of my favourite walks are in woodland settings nearby, and I often take my camera with me. Marry this with my fascination and love of fairies and you can see where the inspiration for this project sprang from. My imagination leads to images of fairies hiding under wild mushrooms, taking shelter from the rain under large dock leaves and peering from behind a tree trunk. This is quite aside from the beauty that can be found in nature itself, thereby creating an inner feeling of joy which can in turn be translated into a project such as this.

As mentioned, the collection to which this project belongs consists of a series of costumes that are all worked in various media, made with lots of different techniques. These include wet felting and free machine embroidery using all manner of materials: handmade paper, heat-fusible iridescent fibres, and recycled media such as plastic carrier bags, scrap knitting wools, lace, net, braids and threads. I had a world of inspiration already built up from which to draw!

Sifting through the photographs, sketches and paintings I had collected for the original pieces, I added bark rubbings, leaves and other natural ephemera from the woodlands I visited in order to give the piece a central focus.

Design

Materials and techniques

Given the theme of woodland and nature, using natural materials such as wool tops, mulberry silks and cotton scrim seemed appropriate. Using the nuno felt making technique, these could be used to create a fabric that was distressed and textured like that of bark.

Colour palette

The woodland theme made a central palette of green obvious, but I experimented with lots of different hues and tones by making small sample pieces, some of which you can see on these pages. In addition, different colourways relating to bark – in browns, greys and muted yellows – were worked, including mark making sketches resembling the texture of knots and gnarls.

A practice piece – worked on dyed green cotton scrim and combining different shades of green wool tops with variegated mulberry silks – proved the colours would work well together. To break up the green, I decided to add bright red needle felted berries.

Challenges and development

To suggest the strong qualities of a tree trunk, I decided to work the piece in a rectangle. To add interest, and break up the strong vertical lines, I made needle felted leaves in different sizes and materials and decorated some with free machine embroidery in both complementary and contrasting merino wools. On consideration, I felt the small needle-felted leaves, made using wool fibres alone, worked best, so used these in the final project. This resulted in a textured piece which I feel is best displayed as a wall hanging.

In order to make the most of the wall hanging concept, I decided to leave dangling 'roots' of twisted lengths of merino wool at the bottom of the piece. This adds life to the piece and gives a nice finished bottom edge to the project. Very often in nature roots are exposed – the very life of the tree revealed – yet in those same roots lies great strength and stability.

Key guidelines

- Use natural materials to help to evoke the theme.

- Use naturalistic, pleasing colours that reflect the autumnal season you are portraying.

- Lay out all your fibres and embellishments in one direction to suggest the theme of a tree trunk.

- Remain loose and free when laying out your additions to the felt, and do not be too precise or formulaic.

- Keep the berries fairly small and in context with the work.

- Do not over needle felt your leaves – we want to retain an organic, soft quality.

- When attaching the leaves to the base panel, leave the edges free so that you can gently lift them upwards. This will give a three-dimensional effect to the finished piece.

- Remember that this work has an organic theme and, as such, soft lines and free natural edges are wholly appropriate.

WHAT YOU NEED

- Basic felt making equipment: 50 x 50cm (19½ x 19½in) bamboo mat, soap, spray bottle, towel, plastic sheeting and netting
- Cotton scrim: green
- Merino wool tops: cool green, yellow-green, light green, dark green and red
- Mulberry silks: variegated bronze-blue, variegated light pastel
- Cotton mohair wool: green
- Plastic carrier bag
- Felting needle and felting pad
- Embroidery scissors

Laying out the wool

1 Put a towel on top of plastic sheeting to protect your table surface. Cut a 39 x 31cm (15¼ x 12¼in) rectangle of green-dyed scrim cloth. Wet the cloth, then place it on top of your rolling mat, on top of the towel. Cover the whole surface with a fine layer of cool green merino tops, with the fibres running from right to left.

2 On the right-hand side, add some extra merino wool extending off the side. This will eventually be the bottom of the piece, and will become suggestive of the tree roots.

3 Lay some yellow-green merino tops over the surface. Work fairly randomly, letting your eye lead you where it looks best. Once finished, lay smaller amounts of both light and dark green over the surface. Draw these additional pieces out a little to create long, thin stripes.

4 Add a few long strands of variegated bronze-blue and variegated light pastel mulberry silks, and also some strands of green cotton mohair wool. Again, draw them out into long strands.

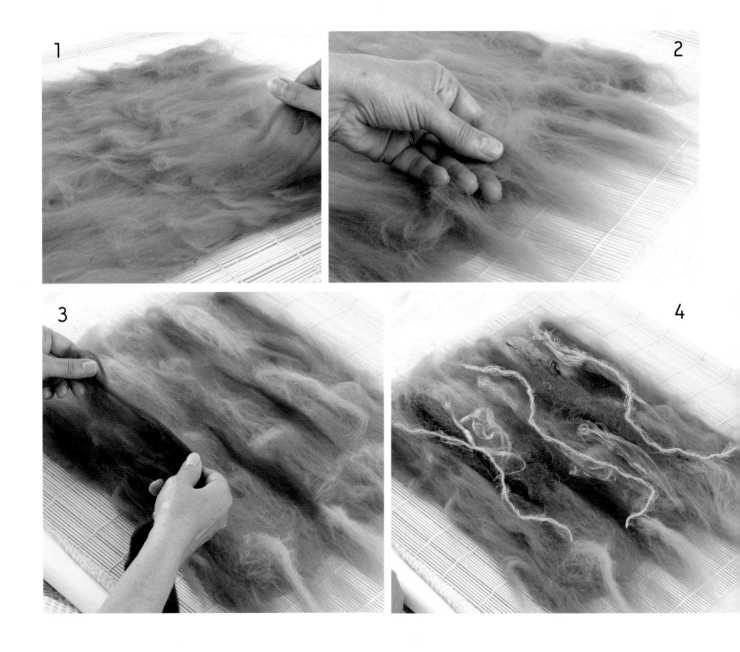

Starting the wet felting

5 Tease out some fine strands of yellow-green merino wool and lay them over the surface to help secure the other pieces, then lay a net – large enough that it covers the whole piece – over the top and wet the entire surface thoroughly. Use a scrunched-up plastic carrier bag to rub over the surface in long strokes from left to right. This helps to distribute the water evenly over the surface.

6 Peel the net back from the right-hand side and pull the roots away from the netting (see inset) before twisting them together to form root shapes.

7 Lay the net back over the roots, then rub soap over the surface in long strokes from left to right.

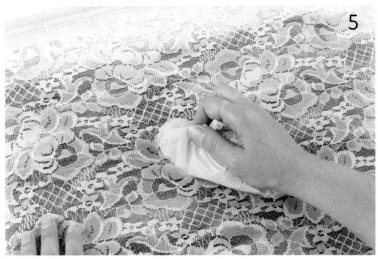

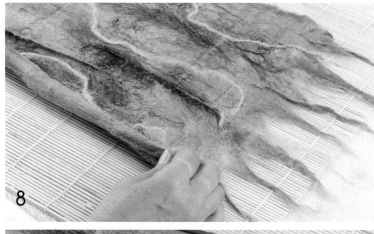

8

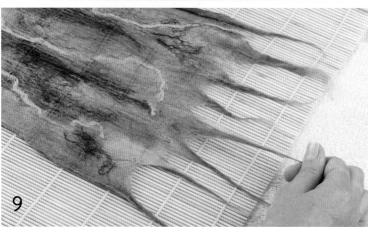

9

10

Nuno felting the body

8 Following the instructions for nuno felting (see pages 34–37), roll the mat up and begin to felt the piece. When you come to remove the net, fold over the fibres on the nearest and furthest sides, leaving the roots and opposite side as shown.

9 Continue felting the piece using the nuno felt technique. Do not turn the piece as you work. Depending on the size of your rolling mat, you may need to move the piece to the left and right in order to ensure the roots and opposite side are felted. As you work, occasionally separate the roots and retwist them to ensure they do not felt together.

10 Continue felting until the roots are felted together fairly firmly. To keep the roots distinct, we cannot felt this in our hands in a rough ball. Instead, fold the main part up into a parcel, avoiding the roots and leaving them exposed, as shown.

11 Pick up the parcel and felt this section only in your hands by rubbing it vigorously. Felt the piece to around 21 x 31cm (8¼ x 12in) (note this does not include the roots, which should add an extra 10cm (4in) to the height), then rinse it and put it to one side to dry.

11

Embellishing: needle felted leaves

12 Draw a small amount of yellow-green tops from your wool, then twist the ends to form the piece into a loose leaf shape.

13 Place the leaf shape on your needle felting pad. Following the instructions on pages 38–39, needle felt around the edges of the shape to establish it and hold it lightly in place.

14 Once the edge is established, continue needle felting the whole leaf, adding small wisps of the same yellow-green merino wool to thicken the piece, if necessary.

15 Once the basic leaf has taken shape and begun to felt substantially, twist a small piece of contrasting wool – dark green here – and place it running down the centre as the central vein.

12

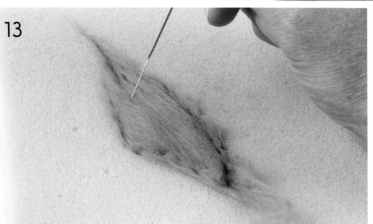

13

14

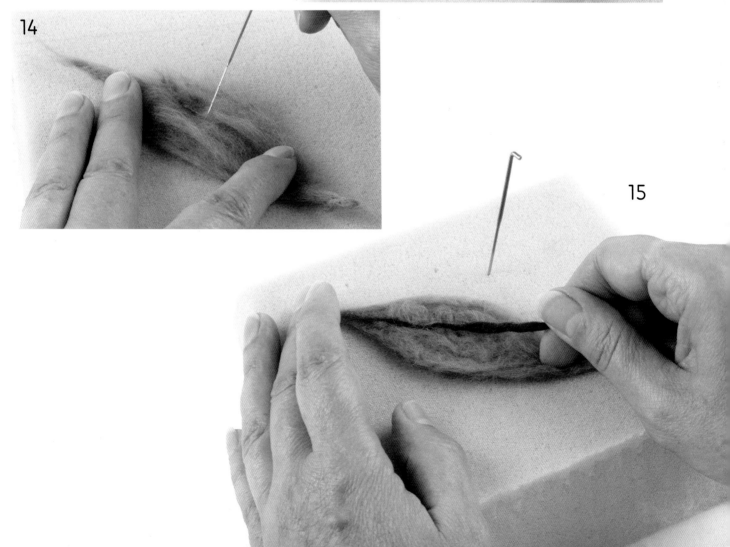

15

16

17

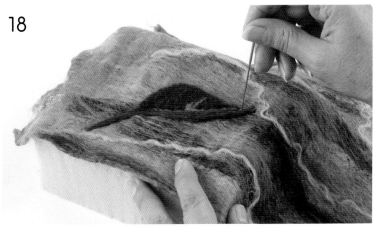

16 Needle felt the dark green wool in place as a central vein, then add some smaller detailing veins in the same way to finish the leaf.

17 Make a total of seven leaves using the different colours of green merino wool.

18 Place the main piece over the needle felting pad, put the first leaf on top in place, then secure it in place by needle felting down the central vein.

19 Secure the other leaves in the same way, arranging them as you please.

18

19

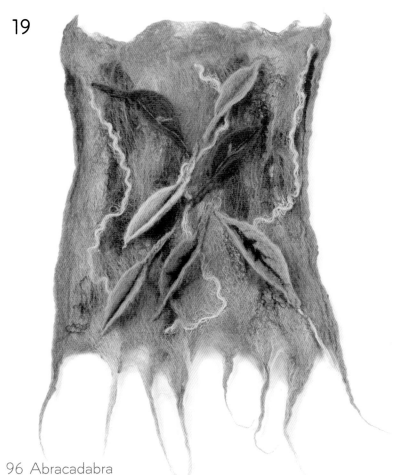

Embellishing: needle felted berries

20 Tease off a small piece of red merino tops and roll it into a ball in your hands.

21 Lay the main piece over the needle felting pad and secure the red ball in place as a berry. Work into the ball to tighten it up.

22 To finish the piece, add around a dozen or so berries in total using the red merino and the needle felting technique. Keep them more towards the centre of the piece, and vary them in size. The finished artwork can be seen on the following pages.

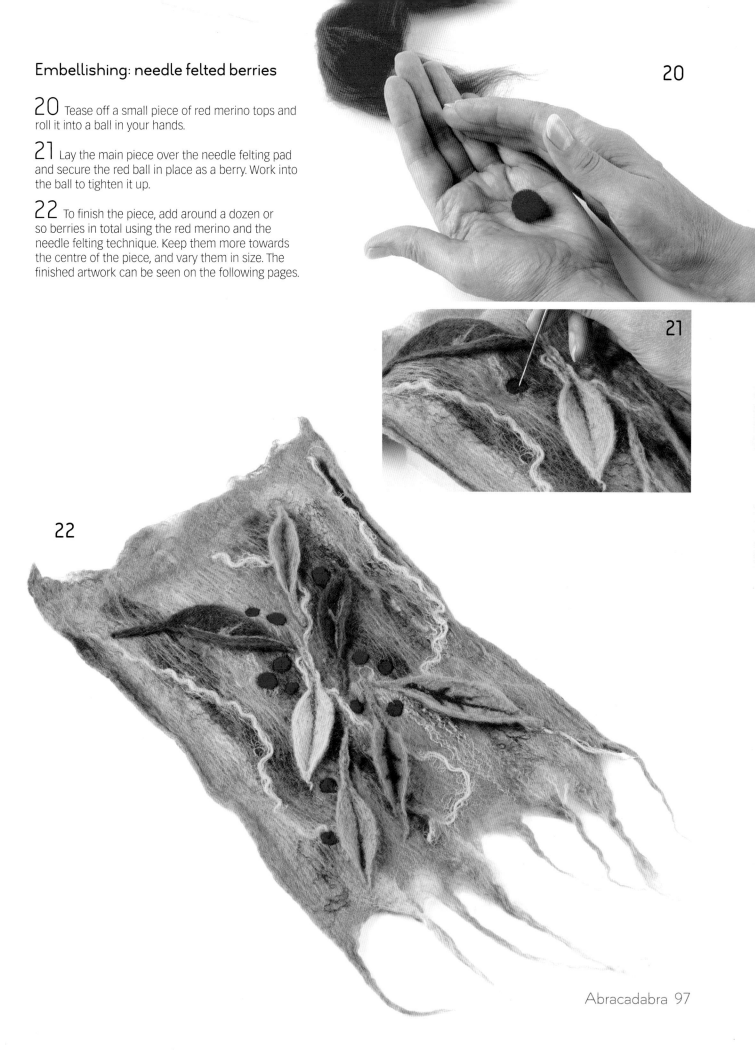

20

21

22

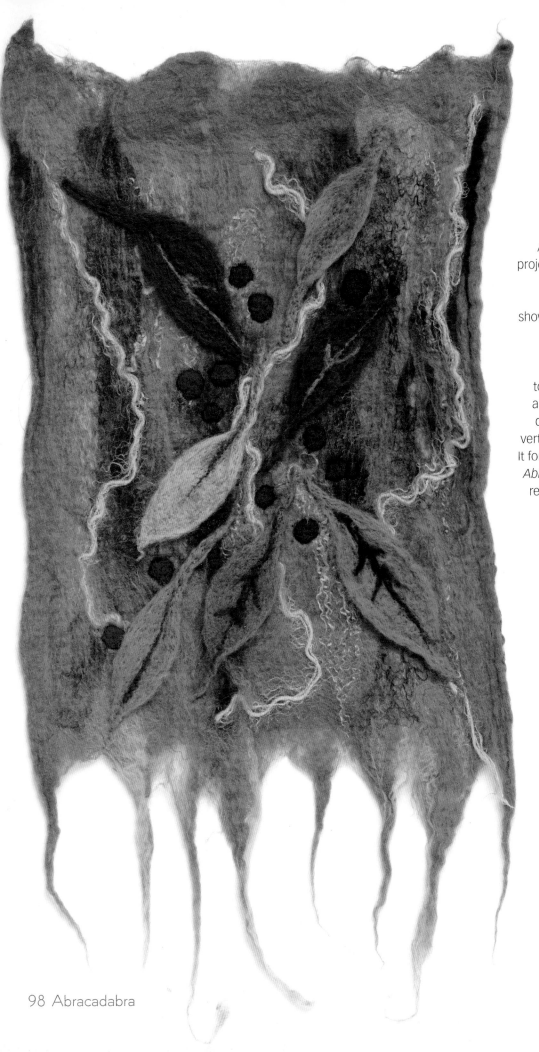

The finished piece

Alive and well! The finished project has a clear appearance of autumnal tree bark with leaves and berries; which shows the versatility of texture you can suggest with felt. Nuno felt and needle felt techniques are combined together with mulberry silks and knitting wool which add definition and create strong vertical lines just like tree bark. It forms a fitting addition to the *Abracadabra* collection which reflects the themes of myths, fairies and transformation.

Detail of leaves

A three-dimensional appearance is achieved by needle felting the middle section of the leaf only, which allows the edges to still be lifted. This gives a distinct sense that the leaves are falling.

Detail of berries

Bright red berries brighten the work and draw the eye, adding to the sense of autumnal change. Needle felted into place, the initial merino wool balls that created the berries remain distinct from the rest of the work, while still forming an integral part of the finished scene.

Woodland

This piece plays with the idea of transformation by adding sparkle and magic to old plastic carrier bags, leftover threads and old knitting wools.

Using heat-fusible iridescent fibres, felting techniques, imagination and creativity to enliven the unpromising materials, the result is an item of fun, wearable art inspired by woodland fairies and tree bark. Fused together using an iron and baking parchment, the piece is further enhanced with both straight and zigzag stitches worked on my sewing machine. Gold metallic embroidery thread was used for this as well as metallic hand embroidery thread, which was couched into place. The knitting wools, left dangling at the hem, add colour and texture.

Whilst pursuing the *Abracadabra* collection, a particular woodland walk made the theme especially important to me. At the time of writing, I am already working on another variation; constructing lots of strips of fabric, threads and other found materials in woodland shades in order to add to the collection.

Opposite:

Woodland

Photographed in an appropriate environment of wild flowers, trees and foliage Woodland is shown at its best here. The colours and shades of the costume and natural surrounding scomplement each other perfectly!

Detail of layering

This close-up photograph of a section of Woodland clearly shows how the layers of discarded and found materials have been gradually built up into something rich, similar to how a woodland or forest floor becomes covered with layers of leaves, needles and other natural detritus. In fact, the piece as a whole was largely inspired by the wooded environment, including trees, bark, twigs, fallen leaves, pine cones, acorns and wild flowers.

Moonglow

This work began very differently to the final piece seen here. The piece itself was constructed, deconstructed and reconstructed. It began life as a previous project – a handmade paper bodice – along with a skirt, partially stitched strips of torn organza fabric, voile and organza ribbon. Never really happy with the first result, I decided to take it apart. My sister Carol helped to tear the paper bodice into thin strips. We then painstakingly stitched all the strips together, including the paper and some knitting wool left spare from a previous project.

The rejuvenated final piece was inspired by a poem I once read about fairies and an illustration from the same book. I imagined fairy feasts in the woods, dancing and singing under the moonlight.

Details of structure

The details on this page show how the handmade paper has been attached to the base fabric using gold metallic thread and a wavy stitch. You can also see the darker-coloured knitting wool, which adds definition to the work. Below this, torn strips of fabric are evident. The distressed and errant fibres and threads are left loose, giving a natural and organic appearance to this fairy costume that helps to tie it in with the rest of the Abracadabra collection.

Moonglow

The ethereal, fairy-like appearance and the vibrant colours add to the overall effect of this work.

I was much happier with this result than the earlier pieces that were destroyed in its creation – not least because it follows the mantra of 'construct, deconstruct, reconstruct', but also because it so beautifully encapsulates the theme of fairies in the woods and forest.

Taken against a stark black background, this image evokes thoughts of midnight under a full golden moon, with gleeful tiny winged creatures whose cares are left far behind!

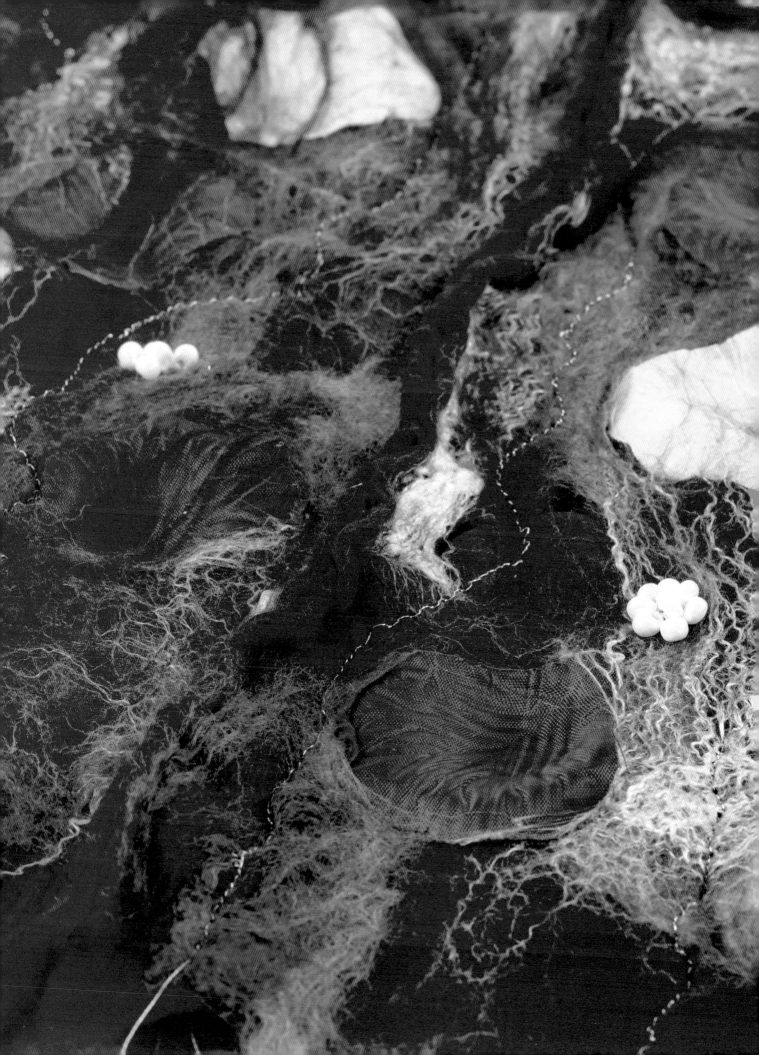

Elizabeth Woodville

Another historical figure I have enjoyed researching over the years, Elizabeth Woodville was born around 1437 to Sir Richard Woodville and Jacquetta of Luxembourg. Around 1452 she married Sir John Grey of Groby in Leicestershire, a Lancastrian soldier who died at the Second Battle of St Albans at the hands of the Yorkists in 1461. Later she became mistress to King Edward IV of England – himself a Yorkist – who she then went on to marry in secret. She was crowned queen on 26th May 1465. Elizabeth Woodville is seen by many historians as an enchantress and a sorceress who bewitched Edward. Many consider her to have been manipulative, caring only for the advancement of her family – and indeed herself. Others believe that she was simply beautiful and that Edward, already known as a womaniser, could not resist her.

Elizabeth Woodville's life during the most significant years of the Wars of the Roses certainly makes her a figure of importance. She endured many turbulent years of suffering and struggling through the political intrigues during her life at court, as well as incarceration and years spent in sanctuary. She was also sister-in-law to King Richard III, grandmother to King Henry VIII and mother to the ill-fated Princes in the Tower!

Unlike some of the other collections in the book, the *Elizabeth Woodville* collection is a comparatively small one. It currently consists of just three pieces: a piece of wearable art which you can see on pages 120–121 and two accompanying wall hangings, one of which this project is designed to emulate. The joy of a small collection like this is the potential for expansion. Indeed, developing the panel for this book has further inspired me, and already I am planning ideas and designs based on *Distant Voices in the Wind*. There is little doubt in my mind that this collection is far from finished. Whether the theme will relate to the battles fought, lost and won, or more directly to Elizabeth herself remains to be seen.

'Often I find myself imagining the battles and political intrigues of the past – and the long-gone whispers carried on the wind.'

Step-by-step project:
Distant Voices in the Wind

The project involves creating several strips of nuno felt that are then hand-stitched together with their ruffled edges exposed and their raw edges left at the base of the panel. Following the instructions will result in a striking and distinctive wall hanging with a wonderful draping quality, capturing the ideas of Elizabeth Woodville's strong feminine influence during the turbulent years of the War of the Roses, as well as the dramatic and horrific loss of blood and life during this period of history.

Inspiration

To research this piece, I spent a lot of time visiting castles significant to the War of the Roses, such as Alnwick, Dunstanburgh, Harlech and Middleham. I also made numerous trips to York to visit sites such as Micklegate Bar, where the severed heads of Yorkists – including Richard, Duke of York – were displayed as trophies of war by the victorious Lancastrians following the Battle of Wakefield. I took photographs, made sketches and looked up information in books and on the internet. Throughout, the sadness, horror of the violence and loss of life during this long war remained prominent in my mind, as did the image of the roses.

Another important factor that influenced the collection was the location of my home at that time, which straddled the Lancashire-Yorkshire border. I had always been in awe of the imposing castle at the village of Bamburgh, near the Northumberland shoreline. This castle was a prominent location in the Lancastrians' attempts to hold out against the Yorkists during the 1460s. My family links to this area and this particular castle provided me with much of the inspiration for this piece and the rest of the *Elizabeth Woodville* collection.

Although the work is inspired by a fraught and turbulent period of time, it was important for me to continue to reinforce femininity as a core component of the project. After all, it is based on Elizabeth Woodville, a woman. Given that femininity is a construct that reflects traditionally-cited traits of gentleness, empathy and sensitivity, I wanted both the initial costume and this panel to reflect these ideas. This is why I used nuno felt making for its soft draping quality, ribbons in the dress, beads within the panel and rose petals of course.

Red relates both to the Rose of Lancashire as well as blood loss, loss of life and the injuries sustained. For me it also represents sadness. Elizabeth led a life full of loss: her first husband, her Yorkist husband (the King), her two sons, her mother, her father and her brother, to name but a few. She lost her status as queen and, for a period, she lost her freedom too! I see this as akin to blood loss, a heart that suffered greatly!

'Bewitching, scandalous – a sorceress,
a legend. Rescued beneath an oak tree
from widowhood to queen of England.
A fairytale come true?'

Design

Colour palette

At the core of the design is the colour palette – a striking palette of red and white, to echo the white rose of the Yorkists and the red rose of the Lancastrians. I wanted to include some subtle green touches to represent the fields where the battles took place, but kept these deliberately subtle to avoid detracting from the impact of the red and white. To add some accent colours, I chose purple to represent nobility and gold to represent the fight for the most treasured possession – the crown.

Materials and techniques

I decided to use the nuno felt making process for this piece and worked samples on a variety of materials and including cotton muslin and silk chiffon. Using a traditional wet felting method, I found that a polyester red chiffon worked extremely well. It looked more subtle and had a soft, feminine quality overall. It also gave a lovely ruffled edge, lending itself to working strips that could be stitched together, realising my ideas in relation to the many battles and battlegrounds involved in the Wars of the Roses.

Challenges and development

Petals were an important element that I wanted to include, but natural petals are far too delicate to survive the felting process. I experimented making my own petals using scraps of organza before finding a better solution – I purchased artificial petals which were more robust and could withstand the aggressive rolling and throwing used in the nuno felt making process.

I decided to incorporate pearlised beads to not only add interest to the work but to represent the white rose. I had also seen a portrait of Elizabeth wearing pearls, so all in all it seemed apt.

With the colour scheme in mind, I experimented using acrylic paint, creating mono prints of white and red roses; some with hints of gold to represent the royal houses of York and Lancaster.

I worked other samples that included purple mulberry silk and gold threads to check the colours would work well together. I then moved on to experimenting with free machine embroidery on these samples before making my final decision to use red polyester chiffon, bright red merino wool, hints of green merino, white and red petals of a synthetic fabric, white and variegated mulberry silks in purple and pink together with limited free machine embroidery using gold metallic thread.

It is always worth experimenting. This project, more than any other in the book, is especially experimental. I have selected fabrics and embellishments not necessarily the best choice for nuno felt making (more usually, natural fabrics would be chosen). In this case, the natural fabrics I used in the test pieces had not given me the textures I required for this project and a polyester chiffon worked best. I wanted to create a more subtle and softer appearance to the finished piece, and the way this particular fabric distressed during the nuno felt making process suited my needs.

The artificial rose petals need encouragement. They will not fully adhere to the base on their own, but slivers of merino wool tops across the petals will hold them in place. The finished work has lengths of twisted merino wool which extends its base. This is an important element of the project, visualising loss of blood during not only the battles but also during various other encounters recorded within the courts of the period.

Key guidelines

- Make a test sample with your fabric to ensure the wool fibres lock onto it.

- Rewet your fabric throughout the felting process.

- Check frequently that the petals are staying in place during the rolling process and that they are held in place with wool fibres.

- This is a delicate piece of work – handle it carefully during the rinsing out and application of the beads.

- Do not worry if the results are not precise or perfect. Part of the appeal of experimenting with the nuno felt making technique is its unpredictability.

- Free machine embroidery using metallic thread often requires a new needle in your sewing machine to help prevent snagging and breakages of the thread.

- Be free with your layout, you do not have to follow my guidelines too precisely.

WHAT YOU NEED

- Basic felt making equipment: 50 x 50cm (19½ x 19½in) bamboo mat, soap, spray bottle, towel, plastic sheeting and netting
- Merino wool tops: red and green
- Polyester chiffon: bright red
- Artificial rose petals: white and red
- Mulberry silks: cream or white, variegated pink and variegated purple
- Metallic thread: gold
- Hand sewing thread: red and white
- Hand sewing needle
- Sewing machine with darning foot or clear plastic foot
- Pearlised beads
- Embroidery scissors
- Plastic carrier bag

Laying out the wool

1 Lay down a plastic sheet and put a towel on top to protect your table surface, then place a 41 x 23cm (16 x 9in) piece of damp polyester chiffon on top of your rolling mat.

2 Cover the whole surface with a fine layer of red merino tops, with the fibres running from right to left. The layer must remain wispy and fine if the technique is to work. Extend extra wool off the right-hand side of the piece.

3 Add some fine wisps of grass green merino tops here and there.

Laying out the other materials

4 Add some strips of variegated purple mulberry silk, some white mulberry silk, and half a dozen white and red artificial rose petals amongst the green areas. Make sure that the point of the petals points to what will be the bottom of the piece; the right-hand side, with the longer, overhanging tops.

5 Drape some very fine wisps of red merino tops over the silk and petals. Again, make sure this is laid out very finely.

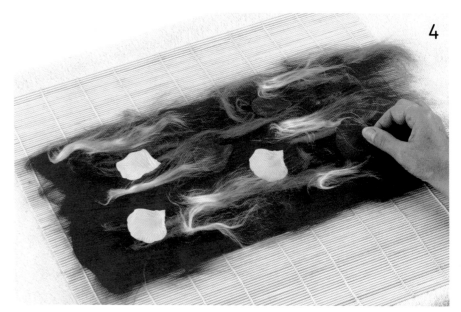

Felting the piece

6 Following the instructions for nuno felting on pages 34–37, prepare to felt the piece by laying a net over it and spraying it thoroughly with water.

7 Because the material is artificial and there are so many non-felting materials involved, it is important that the merino tops do felt well; so once you have put the netting over and sprayed the area thoroughly, rub over more soap than usual, and scrub it into the wool using a plastic bag to force it in.

8 Before you roll, but after you have added the extra soap, peel back the netting from the right-hand side and form the longer fibres into groups by twisting the ends.

6

7

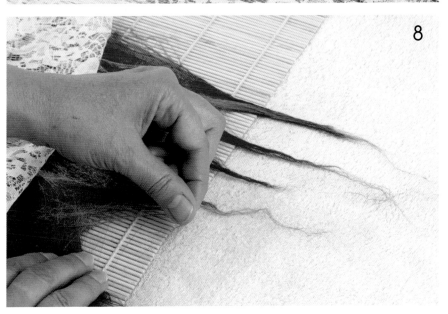

8

9

Nuno felting

9 Replace the netting and begin the nuno felting. Once you remove the netting for the first time, fold the wool round to the back on all the sides except the longer strands on the right-hand side.

10 Artificial fabric dries out very quickly as it repels the water, so rewet the piece before you continue, and throughout the felting process. Use less pressure when rolling, and check more frequently than usual to ensure the petals are staying in place.

11 Turn the piece over every so often as you work, in order to check that the wool is felting into the polyester chiffon. As the wool begins to felt, it will cause the fabric to buckle on the back, as shown in the picture.

TIP: CHECKING

You should be able to see the wool fibres on the reverse of your work. Pinch some between your forefinger and thumb and lift. If the work itself comes up with the fibres, this demonstrates the fibres are coming through the back of the work and have bonded successfully.

10

11

12 Continue felting until the piece measures roughly 14 x 33.5cm (5½ x 13¼in), as shown to the left. If you need to shorten the piece in height, then leave the long fibres at the bottom sticking out of the mat (see above), to ensure that they do not end up being felted into the body of the piece.

13 Rinse the piece out with clean, cool water. Because this technique produces such delicate results, be careful not to dislodge the petals when rinsing it. Instead of wringing the felt out, carefully fold it into a parcel with the wool on the inside, and gently press it between your hands.

14 Make two more pieces in the same way. Experiment with different placement of the silks and petals for each.

Felting artificial fabrics

The results of wet felting are less controllable and reliable when using artificial fabrics and materials. You may find that some of the backing material is visible where the felt has shrunk without attaching to the backing and drawing it with it. An example of this is shown at the bottom of the piece in the image below left (A).

If you decide that you do not like this appearance, you can trim the visible backing away with scissors until it is hidden from view by the felt (B). The improved piece is shown on the right (C). However, do not feel that you have to do this – part of the appeal of exploring and experimenting is the slightly unpredictable results.

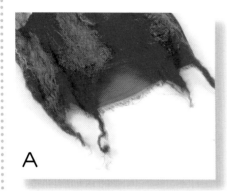

A

B

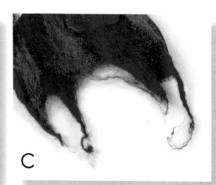

C

15

Embellishing: adding beads

15 Use a needle and white cotton thread to attach small pearl beads in one or two flower-shaped groups across the first piece.

16 Repeat on the other two pieces. You can match or vary the placement as you wish.

16

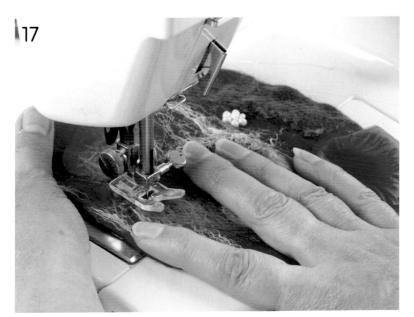

17

Embellishing: free machine embroidery

17 Thread your sewing machine at the top and bottom with gold embroidery thread, then use the free machine embroidery technique (see pages 40–41) to work two or three loose, wandering lines down the length of the fabric on the first piece. Avoid the petals and beads, but you can work over everything else.

18 When you reach the end of the piece, trim the excess thread at the start of the fabric, but leave some trailing at the bottom to help echo the twisted felt. Repeat the process on the other pieces.

18

TIP: FEEDING FELT

Add tension to the fabric in the area on which you are working to help it feed through the machine. This makes things considerably easier for you!

Assembly

19 Thread a sewing needle with red cotton thread and pinch two of the pieces together along the long edges, bringing the backing fabric of each piece together as shown. Using a straight stitch, work down from the top towards the bottom.

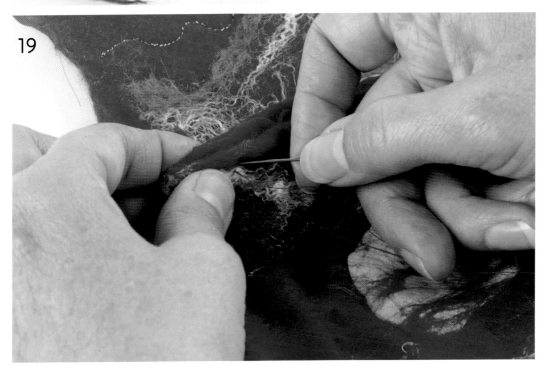

19

20 Work all the way down to the bottom of the pieces. If you find any raw edges of the backing fabric, tuck them in and oversew so they are hidden.

21 Secure the thread at the bottom by taking it to the back of the work, oversewing it with a couple of holding stitches. Trim any excess thread from the back with scissors. Next, secure the third panel to the other two in the same way. This method of attaching the panels together creates a striking ridge between each piece (see inset). The finished artwork can be seen overleaf.

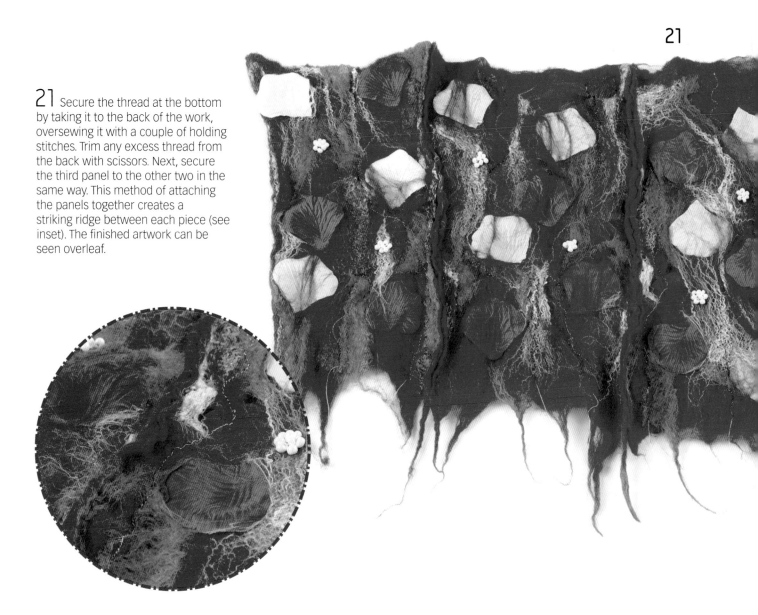

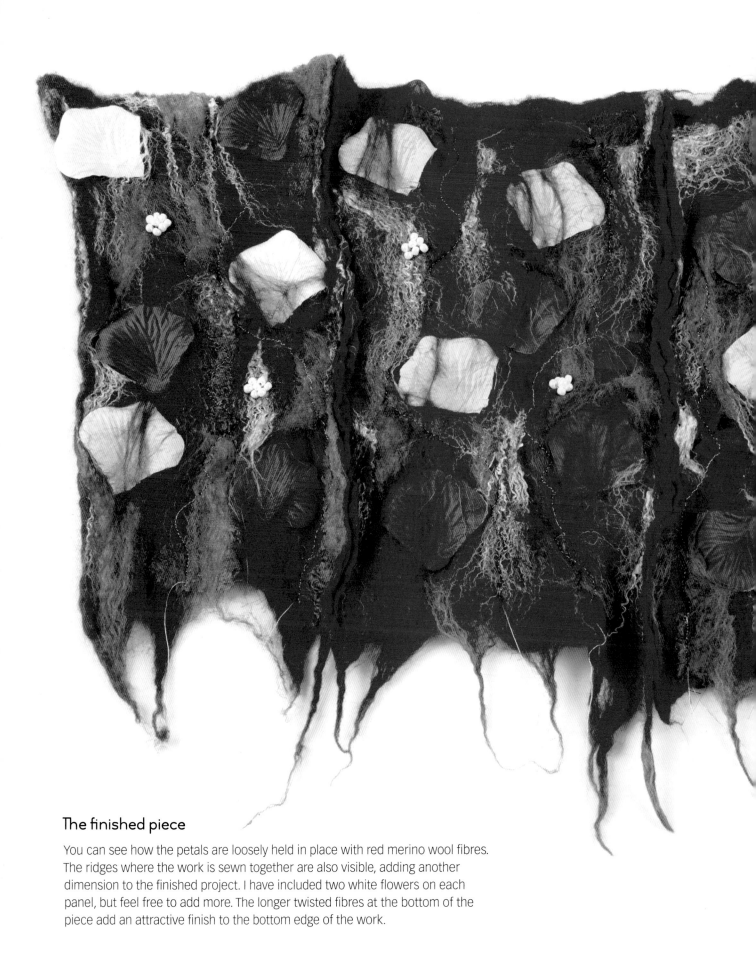

The finished piece

You can see how the petals are loosely held in place with red merino wool fibres.
The ridges where the work is sewn together are also visible, adding another
dimension to the finished project. I have included two white flowers on each
panel, but feel free to add more. The longer twisted fibres at the bottom of the
piece add an attractive finish to the bottom edge of the work.

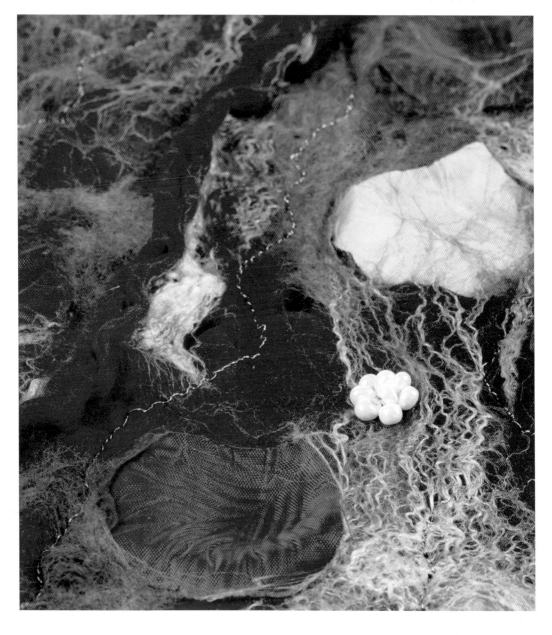

Detail of *Distant Voices in the Wind*

Mulberry silks of white, cream and variegated purple are lightly held in place with barely visible merino fibres, and gold metallic thread can be seen worked in loose, wandering lines. I have added two or three lines to each panel, but the choice of how many to add is yours. You can add more or fewer threads, but remember the metallic gold tells a tale – it reminds us of the fight for the crown!

Wars of the Roses

This wearable art costume was the first of the series which, as mentioned, I intend to develop further. Nuno felted using silk chiffon, cream merino wool and variegated mulberry silks in red, cream and white are embellished with artificial rose petals. These were attached using a similar technique to that within *Distant Voices in the Wind*.

The ridges create separate areas on the dress – symbolic of battlefields – and red ribbon ties on the reverse of the costume suggest blood loss on the part of the warring Lancastrian and Yorkist factions.

Seemingly delicate but surprisingly robust, the dress survives to tell a tale. It has been worn on numerous occasions on the catwalk and hired out for a St. Valentine's ball in London. The petals remain defiantly and proudly in place!

Detail of *Wars of the Roses*

The petals are held in place with wisps of cream merino wool fibres. Red mulberry silk can clearly be seen together with gorgeous textures created using the nuno felt making process.

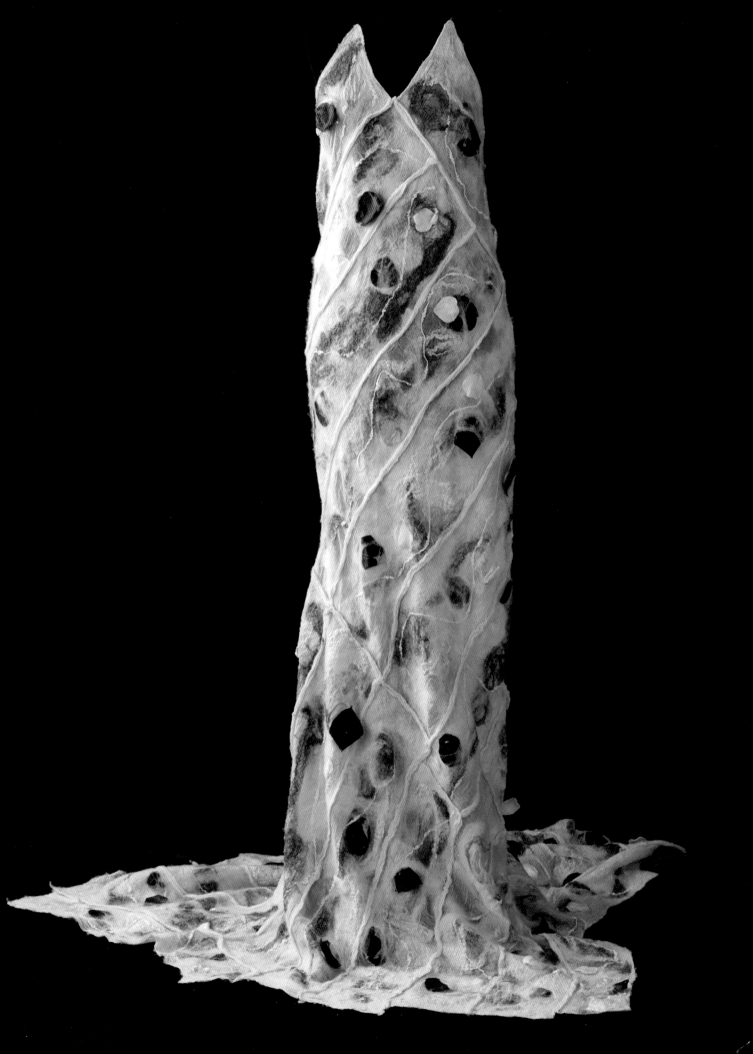

A Call to Arms

Similar in style and construction to *Distant Voices in the Wind*, this wall hanging incorporates more loose metallic thread, more beading and more variegated mulberry silks. It is also slightly larger. However, it still uses polyester chiffon and artificial rose petals.

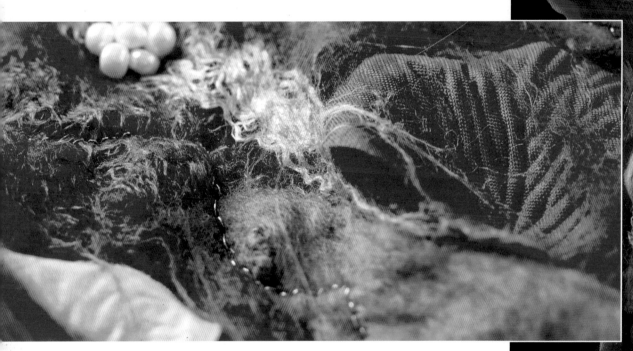

Details of *A Call to Arms*

The texture of the artificial flowers is obvious in the detail above. Green merino wool adds interest and draws the eye but remains subtle. Pearly beads and simple stitching using gold metallic thread completes the picture.

Alice in Wonderland

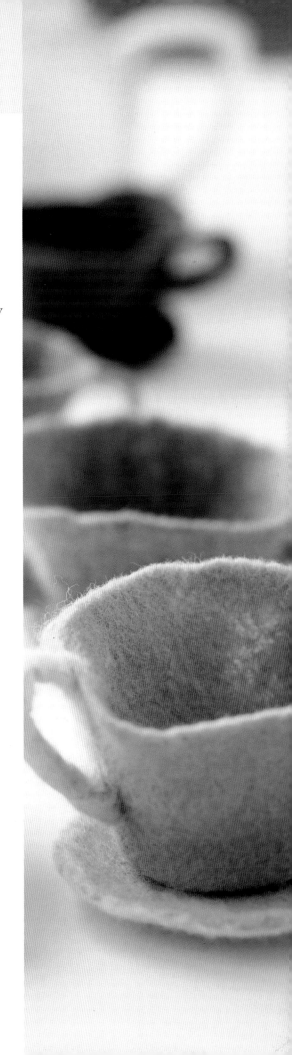

My most recent collection is made up of pieces that play on my childhood fascination with the surreal qualities of Lewis Carroll's Alice stories. Flowers that talk, rabbits wearing waistcoats, white roses painted red, and a topsy-turvy world in which cats disappear and cake has magical properties that can make one grow! The captivating world of *Alice's Adventures in Wonderland* and *Through the Looking Glass* cannot fail to inspire. Characters such as the Cheshire Cat, March Hare, Mock Turtle and the Caterpillar lead us into a world of pure escapism. Lewis Carroll's memorable quotes, wordplay and the sheer nonsensical nature with which he invested his books make these one-hundred-and-fifty year old stories as charming today as ever.

When I first embarked on my Alice-inspired work it seemed to follow on naturally from the themes of my work in the *Abracadabra* collection (see pages 86–103), namely mysteries, magic, and the unexplained, owing to the shared sense of the unexpected. The first piece of wearable art in my *Alice in Wonderland* collection was entitled *Topsy Turvy*. Felted with prefelts, needle felting and lace embellishments, this was quickly followed by a dress incorporating mixed media and text from old Alice books entitled *Curiouser and Curiouser*. In turn, the ideas that *Curiouser and Curiouser* generated led me to making small needle felted flowers, some of which I added to fashion items such as bags and hats.

'I have always felt that there may be a deeper alternative meaning to the story itself.'

Step-by-step project: *Tea and Cakes – A Dream Come True*

Taking direct inspiration from the Hatter's tea party in Lewis Carroll's book *Alice's Adventures in Wonderland*, this panel features tea cups and saucers, cupcakes and red hearts. I have always found the tea party to be exciting, fun and a little bit mad – it always makes me smile and laugh!

Inspiration

I made a number of sketches of the main characters and memorable scenes from *Alice in Wonderland*. Looking back over them, I tried to identify common themes. Red roses in my sketchbooks reminded me of the gardeners who mistakenly paint the roses white instead of red; and tea-stained pages made me think of the continuous tea drinking at the Hatter's tea party.

Food and drink play an important role throughout the story of *Alice's Adventures in Wonderland*. Indeed, as our heroine lands on the floor of the rabbit hole, she is almost immediately invited to eat cake that can make you grow and drink a potion that can make you shrink! The theme is developed in the tea party, so I decided this would form the core of the piece.

I wanted to add a reference in the piece to the Queen of Hearts: the bad-tempered monarch who is quick to decree death sentences at the slightest offence. The Queen of Hearts is, of course, also a reference to playing cards, and I toyed with the idea of including cards before deciding that they would overcomplicate the piece. I decided to include simple red hearts to offer a reference without overstating the importance of the Queen of Hearts.

'It has long been an unanswered question for me –
what exactly was the white rabbit late for?
Curiouser and curiouser! Do you know?'

Design

Challenges and development

For this panel flowers, keys, mushrooms, dragonflies, clocks, playing cards and phrases from Lewis Carroll's books – such as 'Drink Me, Eat Me' – all came to mind. I considered a variety of designs, but my thoughts kept returning to the imagery of hearts, drinking tea and eating cake, so I chose those as my theme.

Part of my preparatory work included creating three-dimensional teacups and saucers and miniature cakes using felting techniques with a traditional simple resist. Needle-felted mice and birds accompanied these creations, but I decided to restrict these elements to just a few needle felted hearts in order to keep the piece strongly themed and remind us of the Queen.

I considered making silk cocoon papers and stitching these images using free machine embroidery, and also thought about adding felt in the shape of cups and cakes, again defining them through stitch onto cotton muslin. I finally centred on wet felting a panel incorporating prefelted hearts and defined cups, saucers and cupcakes.

Materials and techniques

The main base of the piece is made using the wet felting method, but this project also utilises prefelts and free machine embroidery using both coloured and metallic threads.

Part of the fun of prefelts is that it becomes very simple to adapt and rethink the design, so feel free to make your own changes. You might like to include more hearts, more cups and saucers or perhaps an extra cake or two! A touch of heat-fusible iridescent fibres could perhaps add a little bit of magic sparkle to the party.

Colour palette

This project demanded something that was bright, colourful and cheerful – so I chose a broad and saturated set of colours including pinks, oranges and bright red. I chose a bright blue sky and lush green grass to bring us back to the outdoor setting for the Hatter's tea party.

Key guidelines

- Keep to the theme.
- When making prefelts, felt in the same way as you would normally wet felt but do not work it completely. Make sure you can still move the fibres around between your forefinger and thumb. The wool should be felted enough to enable you to cut it but still maintain its shape.
- Take your time. A complicated design like this requires patience to get it just right!
- Be careful not to move your laid-out design when you first begin to rub the fibres and prefelts.
- Adding plenty of water will ensure that everything is held in place. Use your spray bottle only. Do not be tempted to pour water over the design from a jug or kettle as this may result in loss of design.
- Work gradually and check to ensure your prefelts are locking onto your design throughout.
- Remember to reshape the piece every time you turn it otherwise your design will become distorted.

WHAT YOU NEED

- Basic felt making equipment: Bamboo mat 50 x 50cm (19½ x 19½in), soap, spray bottle, towel, plastic sheeting and netting
- Sewing machine with darning foot or clear plastic foot
- Metallic threads: gold
- Sewing threads: pink, red, yellow and orange
- Hand embroidery threads and large-eyed embroidery needle
- Heat-fusible iridescent fibres
- Merino wool tops: blue, green, red, orange, white, pink, dark pink, black, purple and yellow
- Plastic carrier bag
- Dressmaking scissors

Creating prefelts

1 Protect your surface by putting a towel on top of plastic sheeting. Remembering to place each layer at right angles to the previous one, set out a 15cm (6in) square of red merino tops.

2 Follow the instructions on pages 30–33 to wet felt them to the stage that the fibres have begun to bind together. Periodically check the felt by pinching the piece from both sides. It will be at the correct stage if the fibres can be drawn away from each other (see inset), but the piece holds its shape.

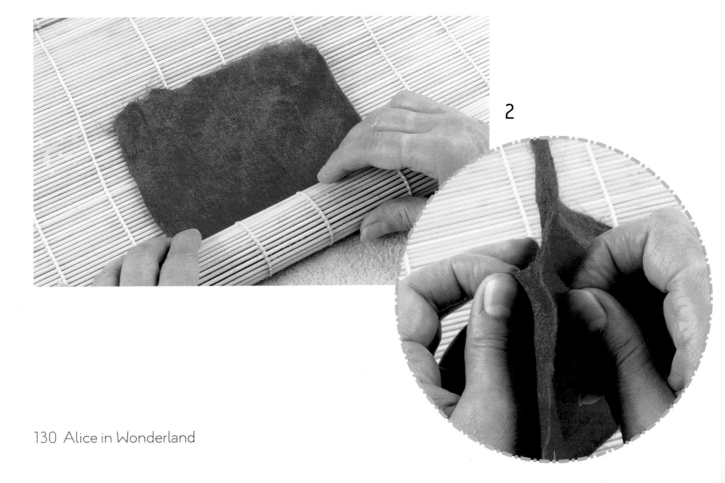

3 At this stage, the material is called prefelt – it is felted enough to hold a shape when worked into another piece, but the fibres remain free enough that they can still be attached to another layer of felt. Use some large dressmaking scissors and the heart template (see below) to cut three heart shapes from the red piece of prefelt.

4 Make a pink piece of prefelt exactly as above, and cut three cupcake case shapes from it using the template below. Put all the prefelts to one side.

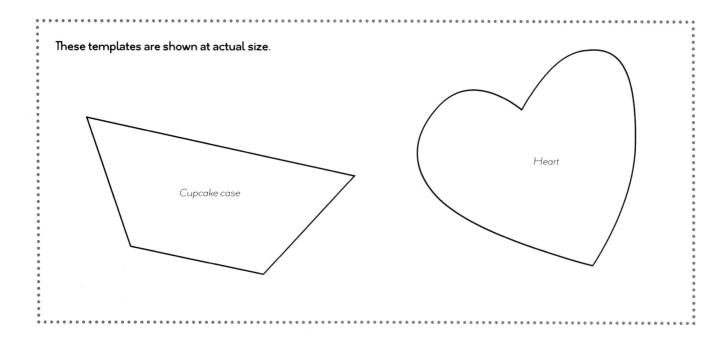

These templates are shown at actual size.

Cupcake case

Heart

Laying out the wool

5 Draw out white merino tops and create a layer measuring 39 x 36cm (15¼ x 14½in), with fibres that run from top to bottom.

6 Draw out more tops and create another layer of white tops at a right angle to the layer below.

7 For the third layer, cover the top two thirds with blue merino wool and the bottom third with green merino wool, both laid with the fibres running from top to bottom. Wrap the coloured wool around the white edges of the lower layers (see inset) to ensure you do not end up with a white border on the finished piece.

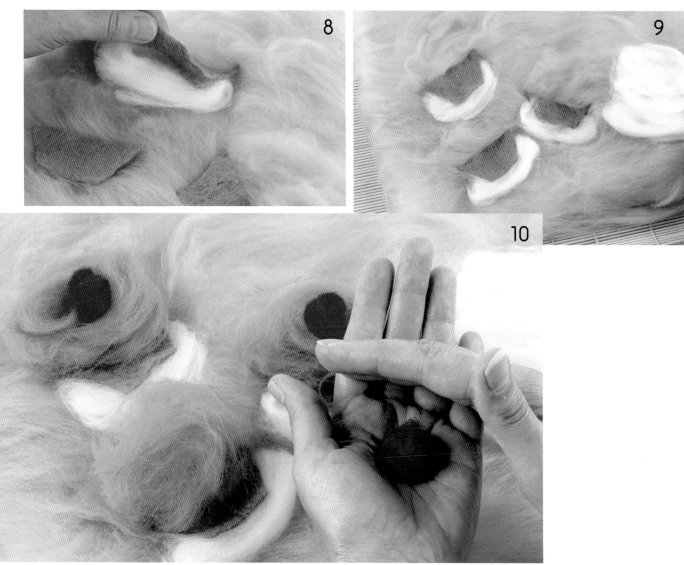

Assembly

8 Place the three cupcake case prefelts on the lower left-hand side of the main piece. Once you are happy with the placement, draw off some pure white merino tops, tease them into the shape of plates and place them beneath the prefelts.

9 Add a cup and saucer shape on the lower right-hand side of the main piece, using pure white merino tops. For the cup handle, twist the ends of a small amount of pure white wool, curl it and pop it in place.

10 Use orange merino tops to add the icing on the cakes, then roll small amounts of red merino tops in your hands to make three small cherries. Place one on the top of each cake.

11 Use the same rolling technique to make tiny balls of pink merino wool. Use these to decorate the plates and saucer. Do the same with purple and yellow merino tops to add some flowers across the green area.

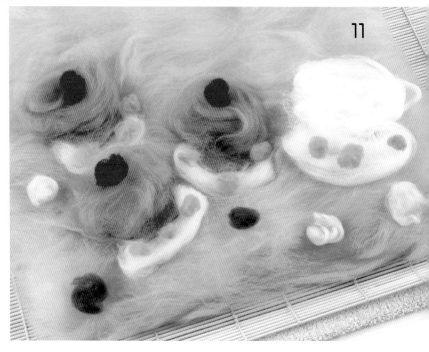

12 Draw out long, fine fibres from the black merino tops and twist them tightly into twists. Use these to add outlines around the cup and saucer and to add detail to the cupcake cases.

13 Use some yellow twists to add some tea in the cup, some steam rising from the cup and some texture on the cupcake icing. Add detail by adding a pink twist to the closest saucer and some pink balls to the cup.

14 Place the heart prefelts in the sky area.

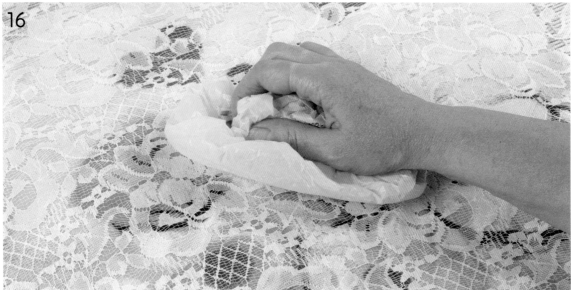

Felting the piece

15 Cover the whole piece with netting, wet it thoroughly with the spray bottle, and draw the soap across it all.

16 For a complicated design like this, it is particularly important that the soapy water holds everything in place, so drive it deeply into the piece by rubbing over the surface with a plastic bag. Re-wet, add more soap, and repeat.

17 Roll the whole piece up tightly, then begin wet felting the piece, as described on pages 30–33. Work more gradually than usual – perhaps every twenty-five rolls or so, then unroll it, peel back the netting carefully and check that the pattern is holding in place.

18 The distortion that happens as you felt a piece will be particularly marked, so reshape the piece every time you turn it; and remember to work gradually. Pay particular attention to the prefelt shapes, rewetting and adding soap if necessary to help them adhere.

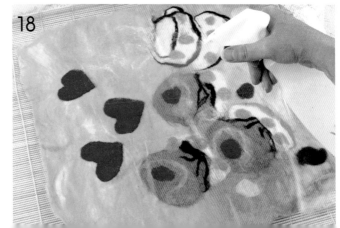

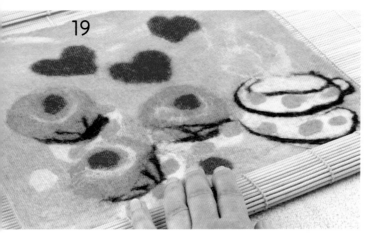
19

20

19 Continue felting the design gradually until the piece measures approximately 31 x 31cm (12 x 12in).

20 Rinse the piece in clean water, wring it out, then reshape and allow to dry naturally.

21 Thread the top and bottom of your sewing machine with gold thread. Following the instructions on pages 40–41, use the free machine embroidery technique to add a gold inner border to each of the hearts. Oversew to secure each one, and trim any excess thread.

22 Use the same technique to add petal shapes over all of the purple and yellow flower areas in the grass at the bottom of the piece.

21

TIP: METALLIC THREAD

Metallic embroidery thread can be quite fragile, but it is worth persevering with it to achieve the wonderful results. If your thread is snapping very frequently, try adjusting the tension on the lower spool of your sewing machine, or working more slowly.

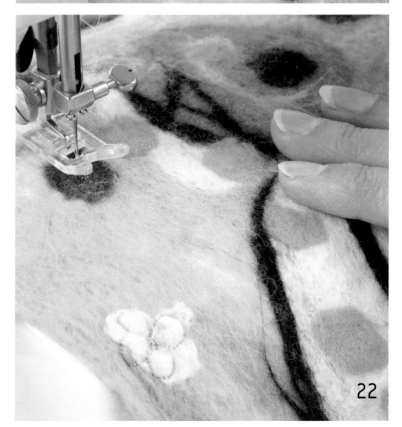
22

23 Use gold thread and the free machine embroidery technique to add details to the icing on the cupcakes, the plates and the cup. Add some wavy gold lines coming from the tea to suggest steam.

24 Add more free machine embroidery detailing with some other complementary threads. Here, I have used pink embroidery thread to highlight the borders and decorations on the plates and saucers, and red embroidery thread to add some swirls on the cherries on the cupcakes.

25 Referring to page 79 for the technique, use a large-eyed needle and short lengths of yellow and orange cotton thread to add French knot embellishments in the centres of the flowers and in groups around the cherries. The image below right shows the positioning, and there are more images of the finished artwork on the following pages.

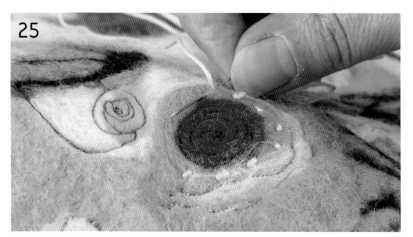

The finished piece

Inspired by my first creation in the *Alice in Wonderland* collection, this fun and
vibrant piece utilises lots of colour to set off the slightly abstract and distorted
cupcakes and crockery. Together with bright red hearts, which bring a contrasting
highlight to the sky, pretty flowers are incorporated near the bottom of the work,
adding to the sense of outdoors.

Detail of cake and heart

Adding free machine embroidery to felt gives it a wonderful three-dimensional lift. Suddenly the cakes become more scrumptious and highly edible-looking. Free machine embroidery also helps to define shapes – this is particularly noticeable on the heart, which no longer lies flat amongst the blue sky but instead is slightly raised.

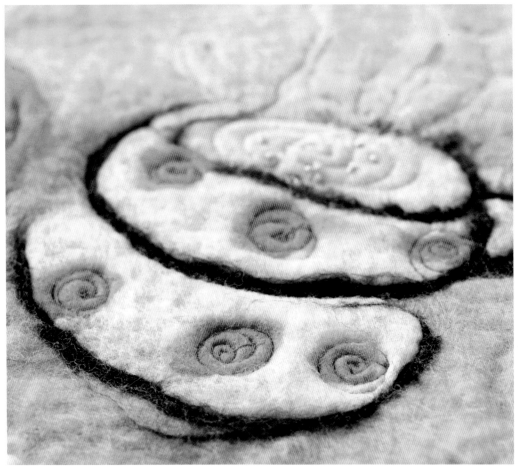

Detail of cup and saucer

A nice hot cup of tea! Steam rises from the cup in the form of yellow merino wool fibres embellished with wavy lines of metallic gold thread. Pretty decorated cups outlined with black twists of merino wool fibres. Pink merino and free machine embroidery adds a design element to the cups and saucers. French knots of yellow hand embroidery thread add detail and texture to the lovely cup of tea itself.

Topsy Turvy

A fun and decorative piece of artwork, this piece was designed to kick-start my *Alice in Wonderland* collection. I chose blue because Alice is often depicted wearing a blue dress. I also chose to incorporate lace to evoke the Victorian period when the book was first published. The addition of lace seemed to complement the felted costume.

Worked in a very similar way to the project piece, the costume incorporates prefelted cupcakes, cups and saucers and red heart shapes. In addition, I added hand-embroidered daisies relating to Alice's outdoor adventures both leading up to her fall down the rabbit hole and into Wonderland itself.

Unlike the project, I have not added free machine embroidery to the design as I felt that the work was busy enough anyway.

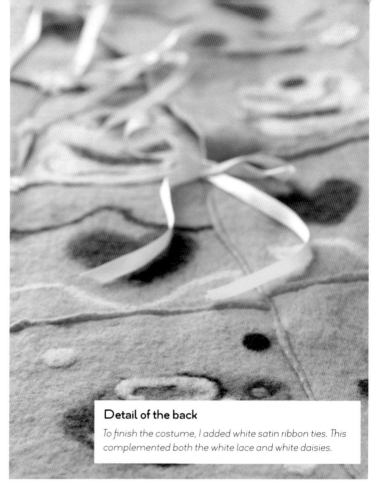

Detail of the back
To finish the costume, I added white satin ribbon ties. This complemented both the white lace and white daisies.

Detail of *Topsy Turvy*

Lots of hearts in various sizes embellish the work, with some being outlined with twists of both black and white merino wool.

Curiouser and Curiouser

The second piece of wearable art in the collection, I wanted to achieve a dreamlike quality with some things clearer than others to the eye. The quirky design and unusual materials aim to celebrate the fun elements within Lewis Carroll's stories.

The basis of *Curiouser and Curiouser* is mixed media – mainly blue plastic carrier bags, but incorporating scraps of text from old copies of *Alice's Adventures in Wonderland*, and handmade paper made from silk cocoons, scraps of lace, fabric and knitting wools. Heat-fusible iridescent fibres help to keep everything in place. Like *Topsy Turvy*, I used lace to finish the bodice and hem of the costume.

Detail from *Curiouser and Curiouser*

Pink iridescent heat-fusible fibres can be clearly seen in the image above. These add brightness to the work and help to give it a visual lift.

Detail of *Curiouser and Curiouser*

This close-up photograph of a section of the fabric shows the randomness of the piece. To achieve this, I worked quickly and freely, adding text, fibres and other additions randomly and without too much precise thought.

Detail of the reverse

This photograph shows the reverse of the costume, with lace ties providing a neat and practical finish to the dress.

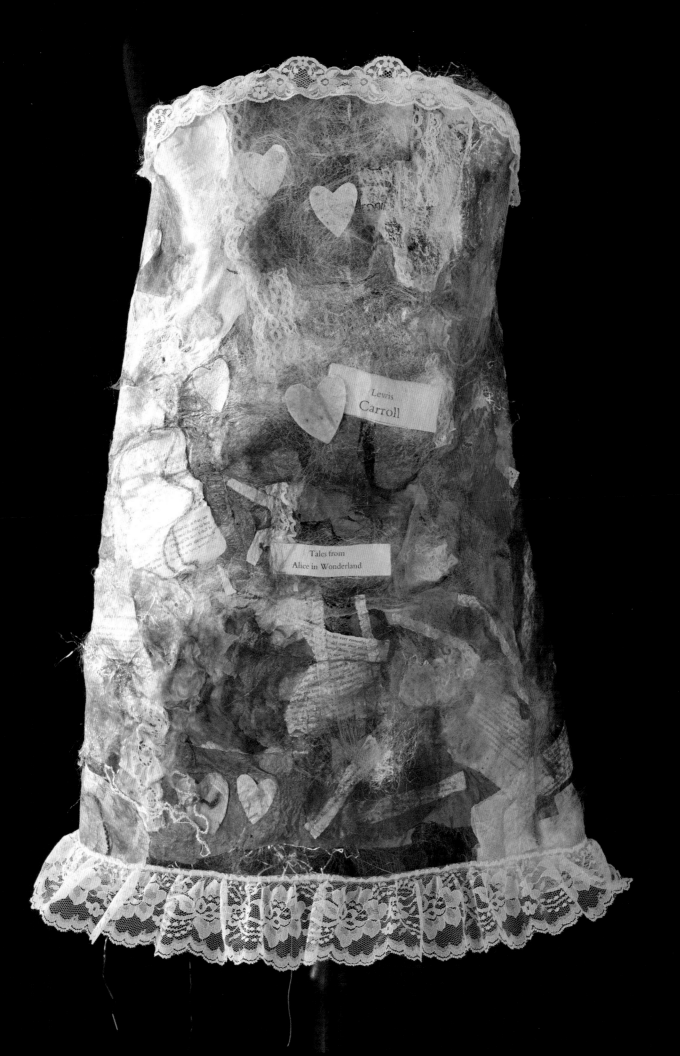

Lewis
Carroll

Tales from
Alice in Wonderland

Index

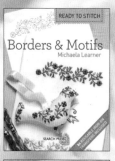
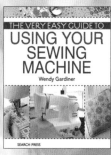

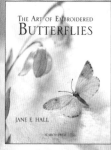

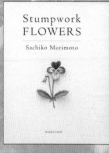

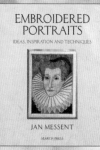